THE SOUL OF SOUTHERN COOKING

THE SOUL OF
SOUTHERN COOKING

By Kathy Starr

Edited by Roberta Miller
Illustrated by Eugene Ham

Foreword by Vertamae Smart Grosvenor

University Press of Mississippi
Jackson and London

Library of Congress Cataloging-in-Publication Data

Starr, Kathy.
    The soul of southern cooking / by Kathy Starr.
    p. cm.
    ISBN 0-87805-421-9 (lib. bdg.). — ISBN 0-87805-415-4 (pbk.).
    1. Cookery, American—Southern style. 2. Cookery, Afro-American.
I. Title.
TX715.2.S68S83   1989   89-36245
641.5975—dc20   CIP

The painting on the back cover was done during an Artist-in-Schools Residency at A.W. Watson Junior High School in Port Gibson, Mississippi, under the direction of artist Brenda Wirth-Schott. This residency was sponsored by Mississippi Cultural Crossroads and funded in part by the Claiborne County Schools, the Mississippi Arts Commission, and the National Endowment for the Arts.

This cookbook
is dedicated to
my grandmother,
Frances Fleming Hunter,
who raised me and taught me
how to cook, so that now
the love of cooking
is in my bones
and in my nerves.

Contents

Foreword

Cookbooks are hotter than a piece of chicken in a black cast-iron skillet of grease!

Cookbooks, like FAX machines and microwave ovens, are things that folks these days just have to have. Some people won't boil an egg unless it's by the book. There are cookbooks from countries we can't even find on the map, cookbooks for every kind of diet and literally every taste. There are books with a month of meatless suppers for steak and potatoes men. Books for Tex-Mex food without the chili. Books on how to put a tang in dishes cooked with no salt, on stuffing fish with fish, and on the 101 possibilities of chicken.

Volumes have been written about "new" regional American cooking. But, like the Gullah proverb, "A 'mos kill bird don't make soup," meaning, in this case, there is still much we do not know about the old American cooking, especially African-American cuisine. Until recently it was not even considered "cuisine" — but just "soul food," a cookery that, like Topsy, jest "growed" from Massa's leftovers.

I was raised in a time and place where we African-Americans were expected to believe all sorts of foolishness about ourselves and our history. We were led to believe we had few, if any, cultural links to Africa. Nobody even mentioned a culinary heritage. Even so, something always told me that soul food didn't no mo' jest grow from Massa's leftovers than a peach jest grows on a watermelon vine.

To make a long story short, in 1959 I was in a market on the Rue de Seine in Paris and saw some foodstuffs that looked familiar. But I was thinking they couldn't be what I thought they were because that was only something we ate back home in Carolina and I wasn't gonna hardly find nothing in Paris that I ate in Carolina. Still, since they looked like what I thought they were, I asked an African woman who was buying some how she fixed them. "Well," she said, "today I am going to purée them, but you can roast them, you can make a tart out of them, you can fry them, you can cook them with a little butter and sugar. . ." My heart fluttered as she talked, because those familiar things were yams, and I realized that she made them like we made them at home. And from that day on, I knew soul food had a history.

It is true that soul food/African-American cuisine is uniquely Southern. Those untold millions of captured Africans brought to the Southland managed, with no cookbooks, to create a true nouvelle cuisine. They came naked to the New World, but they brought their culinary and food memories with them. The cooking techniques and the farming and fishing practices of Yorubaland, Dahomey, Kongo, Senegambia, and other West African nations blended Native American and European influences to make a true Creole cookery.

All praise and credit is due those first black cooks. Imagine being kidnapped from your homeland, taken to a strange place, and told, "cook." Then imagine doing it for the rest of your life. For free. Folks with that kind of awesome culinary know-how deserve more than the condescending, patronizing mention they usually get. When mentioned at all, it has generally been said that they did what they did without knowledge of what they were doing. They cooked like they danced: "from instinct." From an 1880 *Harpers's:* "The Negroes are born cooks, as other less favored beings are born poets."

It was refreshing to read in Evan Jones's *American Food:* "The percentage of slaves taught to cook in a European style is slight in comparison to the number of black women who were forced to make do for their families—

especially in the economic debacle that followed in the defeat of the Confederacy—with roots, beans, fish, opossums, and other wild animals. Yet the food that was prepared in the fields of in slave quarters, regardless of the raw materials, had its own style and flavor because the same food had been cooked for generations in Africa."

If I had to define soul food, I would call it Southern food, a good-eating, creative, imaginative cookery, generous and earthy like the people who created it. I'm not talking about small slivers of skinned chicken breasts surrounded by miniature carrots and radishes cut like roses. I'm talking about *something to eat*. Like a pan of macaroni and cheese, made with real cheese! I'm talking about foods like a mess of mixed greens, fresh greens that you have to pick and clean, all kinds of cornmeal breads, sweet potato pie, pound and spice cakes, and gingerbreads. I'm talking about classic Southern Fried chicken. One of the laments of today is that we have a generation of people who have never fixed or eaten real home-fried chicken.

Soul food recipes, like folktales, are handed down by word of mouth. "How you fix your potato salad?" Since everybody puts an egg in it , that's not the question. The question is: how do you fix *yours*? Because you're only asked when folks think you fixed something good.

My Aunt Zipporah never owned a cookbook, but she could cook the black off a skillet and the white off rice. And she loved to talk about food. She was a living keeper of the culinary records. She knew precisely how much was a pinch and how little was a dash. She could tell when to stir and when to leave the pot closed. She was full of culinary wisdom and proverbs: "Collards anin't no good till the frost hits them." "A watched pot never boils." "If you can't stand the heat, stay out of the kitchen." "We can all hide the smoke, but what you gon' do with the fire?" "Put that on the back burner."

Let's put *The Soul of Southern Cooking* on the front burner and keep it lit! Like Aunt Zip, Kathy Starr is a keeper of the culinary records: "Green tomatoes are better once the frost hits them." "Southerners use sweet milk as the opposite of buttermilk." *The Soul of Southern Cooking* tells us about the integration with other cultures, like the recipe for Mississippi Delta Egg Drop Soup. It's about things we still don't understand, like why some Southern African-Americans ate dirt. It gives us a natural toothpaste recipe and nearly two hundred delectable sho' nuf home vittles.

The Soul of Southern Cooking is a book that will conjure up our Southern food memories any time of the year and tell us about ourselves—*all* of us. Soul food / African-American history is American history, and the more we know about our history, the better we are for it. With *The Soul of Southern Cooking* we can have our history and eat it, too!

Vertamae Smart Grosvenor

Preface

Hunger was something the black family had to conquer, and it was a must that simple foods make a delicious meal. My grandmama, even today, can tell you stories of how proud she felt about her sister Malinda, who could walk up out of the cotton field, find company sitting on her steps, and take a shelf of nothing and make the best meal you ever tasted.

There's a long tradition of making good food out of nothing in my family, who have lived in the Mississippi Delta since it was first settled and cleared for growing cotton in the mid-1800s. After seventeen years in the nursing profession, I suddenly understood, while sitting in church one Sunday, that I needed to use my talent of cooking. The parable of the talents means that God has given us all the blessings of a gift, or talent, and it is left up to each of us to take that talent and use it. The man who did nothing with his talents had them taken away. In searching for my talent, I realized that I had had it all the time. So in about 1981 I started my own catering business on weekends and special occasions.

If I could share with you the many splendid days I have enjoyed preparing food in my kitchen for family and friends and catering dishes for clubs and other groups, you could understand the thrills and joys I have experienced. I have written this book in the hope that you may share some of this joy.

I am lucky to have grown up with my grandmother who loved to cook and who taught me the love of cooking. I thank her for being careful to learn the secrets of good soul food cooking from her mother and for mentally logging family recipes from three generations and passing them on to me. With this book, I show my appreciation to my grandmother for her gift to me, and, in turn, I entrust our family recipes to you.

This is the first time the recipes have been written down. My grandmother and I have never used a cookbook. And I didn't own a measuring cup or spoons until I began this cookbook and had to convert my ingredients to measurements others could use. I guess you could say Grandma and I are "dash cooks"—we use a dash of this and a dash of that. We cook a lot by intuition—like playing the piano by ear. I have tried to put that intuition into words so that you can get the feel of cooking with soul.

This book is written also for those people who say they don't like to cook. In most cases you will find that these people hate to cook because they don't know how. Knowledge and experience in the kitchen are the main factors that limit one's ability to cook. Cooking should never be a horror, but an enjoyable hobby.

In the old days all the food cooked was fresh—vegetables from the garden, chickens from the yard, hogs raised and killed at home. And, in some cases, this is still done. But many modern families don't have the time or interest to raise their own food. So this cookbook will not only tell you how to cook fresh food, it contains recipes and directions for creating that good old-time Southern taste from canned and frozen foods. There are also recipes for giving the soul food taste to such foods as lobster, which I fix with corn bread stuffing.

There are a few secrets of soul cooking that you need to know. The first is the need for simmering time. Simmering is cooking food on top of the stove on low to medium heat and keeping it just before boiling. When my recipes say simmer, it will be up to you to decide if you want to put a top on or not. I usually don't, but this means you have to keep a close watch and add more water if it all boils away. But, whatever you do, *don't rush simmering time*.

The second secret of cooking is really a necessity: *do not leave the kitchen when food is cooking.* My grandmama says if you leave the kitchen you take the air with you and the water goes out of the pot. I know that you just can't cook that way. When you leave the room, you lose track of time and you burn the food. So, when you're cooking, you need to stay right there with it. And that's the truth.

The third secret of soul food cooking is this: before you start using these recipes, be sure to purchase a *black cast-iron skillet*, if you don't already have one. There's something about an iron skillet that makes your fish and chicken crisp and golden brown. You can use your electric skillet or your pretty little aluminum frying pan, but it won't be like that old black skillet. It's not a myth; it's just the true art of frying.

A couple of other types of kitchen equipment are essential in my kitchen—a dishpan and boilers. By dishpan I mean a round white granite pan rimmed in red. The large one, used quite a bit in food preparation, is about twenty-four inches in diameter. I sometimes use a smaller one (twelve inches in diameter) for cooking in the oven. What I refer to as a boiler is also called a saucepan. It has a handle, may be made of aluminum or stainless steel, and comes in several sizes. I use these for cooking on top of the stove and in the oven, too.

You will see that many of these recipes have more fats, salt, and sugar than many doctors today say is good for you. Having made nursing my career, I feel it imperative to warn you of this fact. Those individuals who need to watch their diets for health reasons should reduce or eliminate the salt, sugar, and fats called for in these recipes or use low-salt and sugar substitutes and no-cholesterol oils. You will still have good-tasting food because of the simmering time.

I should tell you also that I sometimes use a teaspoon or two of "flavor enhancer" (monosodium glutamate) to my meat dishes to perk up the taste. Foods today—meats, vegetables, butter, milk—just don't have that old-time flavor. Flavor enhancer seems to bring back the fresh taste to foods that have lost their good flavors through overprocessing, freezing, canning, or farming and preserving with chemical additives. Use of this ingredient is controversial from a nutritional point of view, however, and it is not shown in any of my recipes. Its use is strictly optional; you can decide for yourself whether you want to use it.

I have tried to make these meals easy for you to understand and prepare in your home. It is my every wish that you have a sensational experience with these recipes and that you get many a pat on the back for your splendid meals. But *remember*: the recipes in this book weren't put here to stay—but just to help you with good cooking until you've learned how to do it anyway.

I would like to thank my husband, Billy Joe Starr, Sr., for his untiring support and for missing meals while I was writing. I also thank my children—Billy Joe, Jr., and Frances Denise—for their encouraging words and for carrying on extra domestic tasks while I was writing. Their much needed support provided the strength I needed to complete this book.

Special thanks go also to Anne Chambers and Bill Parkins, of the Mississippi Research and Development Center for their encouragement and direction. I appreciate the help of Arthetta Owens of the R and D Center, who typed the manuscript.

Appreciation also goes to my friend Gene Ham, who was able to listen to my stories and recreate scenes of long ago.

My deepest gratitude goes to my friend Roberta Miller—Bert—who assisted me in polishing the final manuscript. During the rewriting and storytelling times I sometimes wanted to run away from finishing this book. Bert had a magical way of getting things out of me I didn't even realize I knew. She has been an inspiration.

Introduction

My love of cooking started early. I was learning from my grandmama by the time I was five years old, which was in the late fifties. She had a cafe known as the Fair Deal, and it was located over on Blue Front, across the railroad track in Hollandale. Blue Front was a string of little cafes where everybody

gathered on the weekend. It was the only place blacks had to go, to get rid of the blues after a week's hard work in the cotton fields. Everybody lived for Saturday night to go to Blue Front and get a whole- or a half-order of buffalo fish or a bowl of chitterlings. People didn't like catfish then like they do now. As soon as the fishermen came by with the big buffaloes, Uncle Ira would get out in the back and start cleaning them.

The every-Saturday-night meal and the prices during my time were:

Chitterlings and Hot Sauce (50 cents a bowl)
Fried Buffalo Fish (60 cents; ½ order, 35 cents)
Flatdogs (15 cents)
Hamburgers (25 cents)
Regular dinners ($1.35)

My grandmama, who everybody called "Miz Bob," would always start a Saturday night with one hundred pounds of chitterlings and seventy-five pounds of buffalo. Once the people started drinking, the hunger would start, and before 11:00 p.m. all of the fish and chitterlings would be sold out. They would be eating those hamburgers and flatdogs (fried bologna sandwiches), too.

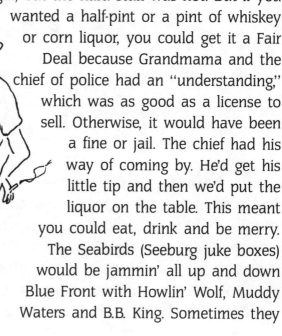

During that time beer was legal, but the hard stuff was not. But if you wanted a half-pint or a pint of whiskey or corn liquor, you could get it a Fair Deal because Grandmama and the chief of police had an "understanding," which was as good as a license to sell. Otherwise, it would have been a fine or jail. The chief had his way of coming by. He'd get his little tip and then we'd put the liquor on the table. This meant you could eat, drink and be merry. The Seabirds (Seeburg juke boxes) would be jammin' all up and down Blue Front with Howlin' Wolf, Muddy Waters and B.B. King. Sometimes they would be there in person over at the Day and Night Cafe. The great blues singer Sam Chatmon came to Fair Deal often. People danced, ate, drank, and partied all night long till the break of day. Saturday night without a fight was not known. But the people always knew that, no matter how intoxicated you got, you couldn't fight in Miz Bob's cafe. If you wanted to fight, you would step outside and knuck it out.

My grandmama served dinner in the middle of the day. She considered it a disaster if dinner wasn't ready by twelve noon. A lot of her

regular customers were farm and oil mill workers. The section workers on the Y & M V Railroad (Yazoo and Missisippi Valley, later Illinois Central) were her regular boarders. They paid her every two weeks when the railroad paid off. The girls at the pressing shop were also regulars.

Every morning about 5:00 a.m. my grandmother would get ready to put the dinners on. I remember crossing the railroad tracks on cold November mornings. The wind would be howling, and the pecans were rattling down on the tin roofs of the shotgun houses. Sometimes you could hear the towboat whistling out on the Mississippi River fourteen miles away. We'd pass the cottonseed oil mill. Whenever it was running, it always smelled like they were making ham sandwiches or cooking fried chicken. The compress was running too, day and night, pressing those bales of cotton. When I'd get over to Fair Deal, I'd crawl up on top of the drink box under the counter and go to sleep to the steady thumping and hissing of the compress. And I'd nap until the good smells and sounds woke me up—big pots of greens and vegetable soup simmering on the stove and Grandma stirring up the corn bread.

My Great-Grandparents

Grandma got her love of cooking from her mother, my great-grandmother, Frances Bolden Fleming, who was known to everyone as Aunt Frances. In the 1890s my great-grandfather, David Fleming, and Aunt Frances sharecropped on the Friley Place, a little way down the railroad track from Hollandale. They lived in a big, tall house set up on pillars, with a dogtrot—an open hallway— through the middle of the house. The house was so high off the ground that a cow could walk under it, and that's where they kept the farm implements, away from the weather. Houses were built up high back in that time, so if

there were floods—which there often were—the houses wouldn't go under water.

My great-grandparents had been born in slavery. They were babies during the Civil War and grew up during the Reconstruction period. Most black families were poor. After the war they mainly made their living from sharecropping. Sharecropping provided black families with bare necessities such as a house that included the rent and some land to raise a cotton crop. In return, the landowner received a share—usually half—of the value of the crop. The sharecropper got the other half minus bills he had run up over the year. Working this way is called "farming on halves." My great-grandfather, like most black farmers, would begin the year farming with high hopes, only to find at the end of the year that he was faced with just breaking even because the rest of his money was tied up in farm or living expenses. If the crop was good, he might make a little money, but most of the time he just broke even.

In later years my great-grandfather ran a molasses mill where he made molasses "on halves": farmers from miles around would bring their sugar cane and sorghum to his mill and then pay him with half of the yield. My great-grandfather had two mules, Meg and Henry. Meg was the buggy mule and Henry turned the pole that crushed the sugar cane. My great-grandfather would sell some of his molasses and keep some for his family.

During that time Aunt Frances had quite a business making lye hominy. She would put it up in jars. It was very popular among many people in the community, and she had regular customers both black and white.

Even though times were hard, Aunt Frances never stopped putting on the great meals. She spent many days canning and preserving vegetables from the garden and preparing for the winter months. Monies were so tight for black families they had to learn all of the different ways for saving. One way was to place items like okra and red peppers on strings, allowing them to dry over the fall. During planting time of the next year the seeds were removed for replanting. Black families really had to learn how to become reprocessing plants. These are the items that were used for reprocessing: butter beans, just dry them out. Peas, okra, corn and red peppers—keep in dry place until spring. You can save seed from all of these for replanting. The sprouts (or eyes) on your sweet and white potatoes can be cut away and replanted for a new crop. The sweet potatoes were piled up and covered with grass or hay. This pile was called a "sweet potato pump" and would last from one year to the next.

My Grandmama

There were thirteen children in the Fleming family, and everybody worked. ed. My grandmama was the youngest and the pet, so when everybody went to the field, she stayed home and helped her mother cook. She would watch Aunt Frances make the lye hominy, and her job was to stay outdoors and keep the hominy stirred with the long wooden paddles. It was always made in big, iron kettles. She also helped prepare vegetables and watch the food cooking, sometimes standing on a chair to stir the big pot of soup on the old wood stove.

Her father's best friend was Mr. Bob Sanders. She was crazy about Mr. Sanders, and when he would sit and talk with her father, she would climb on his lap and play with his hair. He had this beautiful curl that hung over his forehead, so everybody started calling her Bob, and that's how she became Miz Bob.

The older girls in the family had charge of keeping the front yard clean, with the homemade yard brooms. After frost, they would gather the "sage grass" that grew on the ditch banks and the edges of pastures. They would tie the grass around a stick and bind it with rags. Sometimes, they would just bind the grass together with rags and make a floppy broom they just flopped around. Everybody took pride in keeping their yard swept clean. Some people say it was an old African custom. Others think it was to keep out snakes, but my grandmama said it was just because the children played so hard, you couldn't grow grass. The children had to play in the yard. Their mamas wouldn't let them play in the house and get underfoot. And when it was really cold and they had to stay inside, they had to sit still and be quiet.

Another of Grandma's jobs as a child was to polish the silver every Friday. Someone had given Aunt Frances some silver, and it was used for Sunday dinner, particularly if the preacher from Bethel Church was coming. My grandmother polished the silver with a brick. She would rub an old brick with a rag, until some brick dust came off. Then she polished the silver with it.

When my grandmama was still young, she went up to Memphis to live with an older brother and go to school. She got a third grade teaching certificate from LeMoyne-Owen Normal Institute and came home, at age nineteen, to teach in the little one-room school at Percy, out from Hollandale. She would ride down to Percy on the Bigleben train every morning. After school, she would drive back in the buggy, with the principal, Mrs. Bridget Davis.

That was when she married my grandfather, Ed Hunter, a blacksmith. He was very talented in his trade. He decided, since the majority of his work time was spent sharpening the blades of hoes, he would try to develop a device that would allow the farm worker to pull the cocoa grass from the cotton more easily. So my grandfather developed the cocoa plow. During that time, blacks knew very little about patenting a product, and my grandpapa's invention was lost to another person. Many a farmer failed because he could not stay ahead of the cocoa grass.

In 1926 my grandmama became one of the first black postmistresses in Mississippi. It was during the Republican administration of Calvin Coolidge. She ran the post office at Mt. Helena (everybody called it Mound Helena). My grandmama well remembers the famous 1927 flood.

The community around Mt. Helena had been well informed about the flood coming. The government didn't wait until the levee broke to tell people. My husband and I and all our friends spent many evenings moving furniture and house items onto scaffolds we built high up in our houses. The flood waters came by night one evening in April 1927, and, thanks to God, the Indian Mound where my girl friend Henrietta worked as a cook was no more than an eighth of a mile from our house. So we fled to the Indian Mound the night the flood came.

Henrietta cooked for Mr. George Harris and his family, who lived on top of the mound. Although we carried as much food as we could with us, Henrietta cooked for our family just like hers. Everybody couldn't get on the mound, so some families took boats to higher ground and the government provided boats for others. I always thought that the water no doubt, as much as it was, came from some place else. The flood killed all the crops and gardens.

It wasn't long before the Red Cross and the government workers were bringing food supplements to us, like canned salmon, canned peaches, vegetables and Pet milk. Some people ate better when the water was up than when it was down. I was still the postmistress at Mt. Helena at the time. The mail would come up from Rolling Fork by boat, to the foot of the mound. We had a boat tied at the foot of the mound, too, which I used to carry mail out to nearby places.

Despite my grandmama's success in the professional world, which was rare for those times, she decided to turn to cooking as her means of livelihood, and in 1932 she went into the cafe business. She had the Fair Deal Cafe and later Miz Bob's Cafe. By the sixties Mt. Helena at that postmistress at the little cafes were up against hard times. Fast foods were becoming popular, and people were too busy to find the time to eat and visit in the cafes. My grandmama decided it was time to quit the cafe business. Gradually the places on Blue Front closed, and now it is mostly a block of vacant buildings.

Even after my grandmama closed the cafe she still loved to cook. One year, when the cottonseed delinting plant was having an extra busy season, they asked my grandmama if she would cook dinner for some of the workers. So seven of the mill workers came up to the house and ate dinner every day for several months.

Grandmama enjoyed preparing and serving food so much, she encouraged me to go into the catering business. So now I am carrying on the family tradition of serving the good meals.

Pork Preparations
Straight from the Hog

Beef

Soups, Stews, and Such

Wild Game

I like to start the new year off the way I always have, the way all the black families I know do: by eating black-eyed peas and hog jowl, and by shooting the old year out and the new year in. At midnight on New Year's Eve, we shoot a gun up into each corner of the sky—north, east, south, west—to send away all of the old year's troubles and welcome in good tidings and good luck for the coming year. All over Hollandale you can hear the guns going off. Then on New Year's Day you've got to have black-eyed peas. My grandmama believes if you can have your black-eyed peas and hog jowl ready by twelve noon, you'll have a lucky year.

Back in the old days, as soon as Christmas was over and the black folks had settled up with the plantation owner, everyone started thinking about the new year. Some had made a little money, some had broken even, and some had ended up in debt. But always there was hope for the new year coming up. So New Year's Day was celebrated with family and friends.

They'd kill a hog between Christmas and New Year's if the weather was cold enough. Sometimes the men went hunting, but always the women in the family were preparing for the New Year's dinner. This is the menu Aunt Frances and my grandmama always served on New Year's Day, and I still use this menu for my New Year's dinner. It is a different meal from the great Christmas feast, but it is still wonderful and everyone looks forward to it.

New Year's Day Dinner
Black-eyed Peas, with Hog Jowl and Ham Stribblings
Hen/Dressing
Chitterlings
Collard Greens with Salt Meat
Candied Yams
Cranberry Sauce
Corn Bread
Dessert
Lemon Glazed Cake
Pecan Pie

After New Year's everyone would settle down to life in the long winter months, with very little money to spend. In Grandma's time, on sunny days when the roads were dry, the men would take the wagons to the woods and cut firewood. Sometimes they would go to the "new ground" where they were clearing land for cultivation. Sometimes they would go to the "deadenin" where the trees had been girded months before so the leaves and limbs were dead and it was easy to fell the trees. There was always game to be had when the trees came crashing down. Rabbits and squirrels were running for their lives, and sometimes there would be a possum or a coon. Sometimes the men would stop at the plantation commissary or a little country store and pick up a few shotgun shells at a nickel apiece. Back in those days, it cost too much to buy a whole box of shells, so the store owners would break the boxes and sell you a shell or two at a time.

While the men were cutting wood, sometimes the women would gather at a neighbor's house and quilt and sew and visit. They were doing this a long time ago, and they're doing it now at the Senior Citizen's Center.

During the really cold weather, in January and February, everyone stayed inside, close to the fire, as much as they could. When I was a child going to school, I would walk home cold and hungry and ready for a snack. If money was low, the most popular snack was sweetened water and white bread. You would put some sugar in a glass of water, then roll a slice of bread and dip it into the sweetened water. It really tasted good. Another after-school delicacy was corn bread crumbled up in a bowl, topped with sugar, with buttermilk poured over and eaten with a spoon. Aunt Frances would fix this same corn bread treat or tea cakes for my grandmama when she came in from school.

In the old days, after the children finished their snack, they would get busy bringing in wood, splitting kindling, feeding the chickens and stock. When the men came in, they'd unload the firewood, clean their game, and be ready for Aunt Frances's hot supper. Even though food supplies might be low, there were chickens and eggs in the yard, home-canned vegetables on the shelf, sweet potatoes in the sweet potato pump, and milk if your cow was "in." If your cow wasn't in (was dry), you could borrow milk from your neighbor. Then they could borrow from you later on. (When I was coming up, we got our fresh milk and butter from Miss Susie Hunter.) Gardens still had mustards and collards and there might be ham and bacon still in the smoke house. If you needed fresh meat, you could just go out and knock down a shoat (a young pig). People still keep hogs, but greens don't last year 'round like they used to; now they just rot in the soil and go to seed. A traditional winter breakfast then and now is salt pork, homemade fist biscuits, and molasses.

Winter was the time for men to sit by the fire and talk, smoke, and play cards, visit with the neighbors, and talk about the new crop to be planted in the spring. It is the one time of the year when the farmers really had time for a good rest.

If it snowed, which is always rare in the Mississippi Delta, the children were really excited. They could play in the snow and make snow ice cream. Aunt Frances would give everybody a cup or glass, and they would fill it with snow and add a little vanilla flavoring, sugar, and cream. Aunt Frances would sometimes make a custard and bury it in the snow, so it was almost frozen. My grandmama did these same things for me.

Many of my old friends have gone on to other cities to make what they call "a good life" for themselves, but I will always remain at home and carry on many of the traditions I enjoyed as a child.

Pork Preparation
Straight from the Hog

How to Kill
A Hog at Home

From around the turn of the century up to my time, black families have provided meat mainly through raising hogs. During the fall of the year, the hog was put on the fattening floor—a floored, covered platform raised off the ground. Placing the hog on the fattening floor was not only for fattening it to a larger size, but to clean the hog out inside by feeding it corn. After the hog has been on the fattening floor for three or four weeks, it should be ready for killing as soon as the moon is wasting (waning). If you don't kill the hog during the waste of the moon, it will not fry out for fat and the meat will be rubbery.

Hog killing was never a one-man job. Always at least two or three men would come over and help. Hog killing was not a chore; it was fun and excitement and we got to eat as well. As soon as the liver was cut away from the hog, the men would have a pile of wood burning. And they would cook the liver in a long-handled black skillet right then and there. Liver never tastes any better than cooked fresh straight from the hog.

You can kill a hog by one of three methods: shoot him, knock him in the head, or cut his throat. Whatever method is used for killing, you will have to cut his throat and allow the blood to drain for about 20 to 30 minutes. By the time the hog is completely drained, the water should already be boiling. Put the hog into a deep vessel, preferably a barrel, and pour on boiling water, turning the hog vigorously until all hair is picked and rubbed off.

The scalding water loosens the hair for easy removal. If you don't remove the hair while the hot water is on the skin, the hair will return to its original state. You put the hind quarters in first. Then lay the hog on a board and scrape off the hair. Next you put the middle portion of the hog in the scalding water, and do the same thing, and last you put in the head, and when you lay the hog on the board you should be sure to scrape off all hair. When the feet are removed from the hog, you have to "swoon" them, which means that you place the feet over fire and burn the hair off. Then you scrape them clean with a knife. Next you dip the hooves in scalding hot water, and pry the nails off with a knife.

When this is done, hang the hog from a rafter for butchering. The hog has a leader (also called a sinew) in the heel of his hind feet, located just below the top layer of skin. Be sure not to cut into it, as the weight of a hog can be held by these leaders. Now split the hog in the mid-stomach area, from anal direction to the neck. A tub should be placed beneath the hog to catch all of its innards. Now you have your chitterlings, liver, lights, hog maw, and kidneys. Once the hog is completely cleaned of all inner guts, you should rinse the hog's casing (the inside of the hog) with cold water, to remove any blood or material. Once you complete this procedure, take the hog down and cut into four quarters, leaving the head, feet, and tail.

Now the hog should be cut into these portions: two hams, two shoulders, two middlings (sides) for bacon, backbone (for neckbones or pork chops). After the hog is cut up, trim the fat off the ham, shoulders, and head. This is what makes up your cracklins. You can decide if you'd like to cut up the shoulders for cracklins. Some people want the shoulders left whole for hams and roasts, instead of using them for making cracklins and lard. The hog's head, feet, and tail are used for souse. For directions as to how you can prepare each portion listed, see recipes in this chapter.

Scrambled Pork Brains

½ cup oil
1 pound fresh hog brains
2 eggs, beaten
1 tsp. salt, more if desired
1 tsp. pepper

In a skillet warm oil slightly. In the skillet beat eggs into brains, adding salt and pepper. Stir-fry until lightly brown for 10 to 15 minutes. Serve hot with fried saltpork if desired. Serves 2.

Fair Deal's Saturday Night Chitterlings

Chitterlings—hog intestines—are one of the South's greatest delicacies. However, some Southerners avoid them because of where they are derived in the hog. But once prepared, they are delicious.

10 pounds chitterlings, cut into 6″ strips
1 tsp. salt
1 tsp. pepper
2 onions, chopped
1 bell pepper, chopped
½ lemon, sliced
3 quarts of water

Put cleaned chitterlings in a heavy-duty boiler. Add salt, pepper, onions, bell pepper, and lemon slices, stirring them into chitterlings until mixed well.

Add water and simmer over low heat for 4½ hours. Serves 3 to 4.

How To Clean Chitterlings

If frozen, thaw chitterlings the day before. Although frozen chitterlings from the supermarket have been partially cleaned, they are not nearly clean enough to cook. Each chitterling should be checked with your hands from one end to the next end, like you are traveling a straight road. It takes approximately two to three hours to clean them successfully. Chitterlings are never cleaned of all residue. You'll find straws and trash bound up in the fat that is attached to the underside. Remove only dirty fat. Do not strip skin off chitterlings, and never remove any more fat than is necessary. Wash thoroughly.

If you are cleaning chitterlings straight from the hog, you will have to cut them lengthwise before you begin cleaning. You will need a very sharp knife, a garbage can (or a number 3 tub or other large vessel), lined with a disposable bag, and hot water. Place all chitterlings in the dishpan, and beginning at one end of the chitterling, cut along a straight line horizontally from end to end. Have the garbage can nearby so that major portions of excrement can be scraped into the disposable bag. Now follow above directions to wash chitterlings thoroughly.

The name of my mother's cafe was "Fair Deal." Traditional menu on Saturday included chitterlings and hot sauce, fried buffalo fish, and flat dog sandwiches. On Saturday evenings you couldn't dish up a bowl of chitterlings fast enough for your customers. What chitterlings were for the black man in those days was the same as caviar for rich white boys. Chitterlings were known as "poor man's caviar."

Cracklins are a snack like potato chips. You can also use them for cracklin bread. (See recipe on page 142.)

Be sure the hog is killed on the right moon. Probably you will say this is a myth, but it's true. It must be killed on the waste of the moon. The waste of the moon means that the full moon has gone through its quarters and is wasting away. If you don't kill the hog at the right time, the meat will swell up in the skillet, and the fat will never fry out of the cracklins.

How to Fry Out Fat For Cracklins

2 quarts water
1 dishpan full of hog fat and trimmings
1 back-yard cast-iron pot or a dishpan
1 tsp. soda

In a dishpan or cast-iron pot, put in water and add hog trimmings. Cook slowly on low heat for a couple of hours, stirring constantly so they won't glue together and stick to the bottom of the pan. This mixture will cook out to good pork fat. Cook meat until all cracklins cook and move from the bottom of pan and float on top of the grease, which becomes lard. This is a sign that the cracklins are ready. Will serve about 30 to 40 people.

Cured Ham

(without a smokehouse)

2 shoulders
2 hams
25 pounds curing salt
1 quart hickory smoke (storebought)
½ gallon smoke-curing sauce (storebought)

Bacon may be cured the same way as ham. Salt meat is not smoke-cured; it is just placed in the curing salt for 5 days and then is ready for frying and eating or cooking with vegetables.

1. Wash thoroughly the fresh shoulders and hams that have been cut away from the hog. Take a cheesecloth or other soft clean cloth and dry them well.
2. Split the joints and stuff them with salt.
3. Take each ham and shoulder and completely cover ½" thick with curing salt.
4. Place meat in a cardboard box, cover with a cloth or newspapers, and set in a cool dry place (not refrigerator) for 2 weeks.
5. After 2 weeks wash salt away with warm water.
6. Paint with a layer of hickory smoke and a layer of curing sauce. You can brush these liquids on or dip meat into them.
7. Put meat back into box; leave for 2 more weeks.
8. After 2 weeks, the meat will be fully cured and ready for slicing and eating.
9. You can refrigerate meat as desired after this process.

Baked Ham and Fruit Delight

8- to 10-pound ham (cured and precooked)
3 cups water
cinnamon
1 cup syrup or molasses
½ tsp. nutmeg
1 6-ounce can sliced pineapple
1 small jar cherries
½ cup cloves

Place ham in roasting pan and add water. Sprinkle cinnamon over entire ham. Paint ham with syrup or molasses and nutmeg. Use toothpicks to place slices of pineapple, cherries, and cloves on top of ham. Cover with aluminum foil and place in pre-heated oven at 375 degrees. Bake for 2½ hours. Serves 20 to 22.

Ham Glaze

1 cup syrup
1 tsp. butter
1 T. pineapple juice
½ small jar cherries, without stems
½ cup crushed pineapple
¼ cup brown sugar

Mix together all ingredients and spread onto ham. This will glaze a 12- to 15-pound ham.

Battered Hog Maw

4 quarts water
4 tsp. salt
2½ tsp. pepper
3½ pounds hog maw
2 eggs
3 cups milk
4 cups plain white flour
4 cups vegetable oil for deep frying

In a deep boiler add water, 2 teaspoons salt, pepper, and hog maw. Cook for 4 hours or until tender. In a bowl beat eggs, adding milk. Set aside. Mix flour and 2 teaspoons salt. Take hog maw and dip it in the egg mixture, covering evenly on both sides, then roll it in flour. In skillet, brown hog maws and serve with hot pepper sauce. Serves 6 to 8.

To make hot pepper sauce: Heat vinegar. Put red or green peppers in a jar or bottle. Pour hot vinegar on the peppers, filling the bottle. If you stick your finger in it, it loses strength.

Hog maw is the belly or part above the intestines. It resembles the chitterlings, but is a wide, flat, thick piece of meat, whitish in color like a chitterling. It can be broiled or fried.

Remember: you won't be able to eat this today. Tomorrow it's ready.

Remember: your hog's head should be cleaned entirely of hair. Boiling hot water poured on head will allow you to scrape away any excess hair in the ears. Remove brains, eyes, and tongue.

Homemade Hog Head Souse

1 freshly killed hog's head
water to cover the hog's head in large dishpan
¼ cup salt (more if desired)
4 tsp. sugar (more if desired)
1 finely chopped bell pepper (red or green)
½ cup sage
1 pint vinegar, golden-colored cider
⅛ cup red peppers (crushed)
pair of disposable gloves

Follow these steps:
1. Split the hog's head in half.
2. Remove tongue, eyes, and brains.
3. In a big, deep boiler, cover the hog's head with water and cook, simmering over low heat.
4. You have got to cook this hog's head until it falls to pieces, it is approximately four or five hours. Let cool before you handle it. You can, when cool, put on your gloves and remove all of the bones from the meat. You MUST remove all bones.
5. Now you're ready to mix your ingredients. Mash meat until it is fine. Mix in salt, sugar, bell pepper, sage, vinegar and crushed red peppers.
6. Mix well, and place in pan. Cover and let gel in the refrigerator overnight.
7. Cut in blocks and serve, or freeze unused portions. Makes 40 to 50 slices. Will keep in refrigerator 2 to 3 weeks.

Homemade Mixed Sausage

10 pounds ground pork from fresh hog
6 to 8 tsp. salt, more if desired
½ cup sage, more if desired
¼ to ½ cup crushed red pepper
pair disposable gloves

Remove as much fat from your pork as possible. Place lean pieces of the pork meat in your meat grinder, grinding finely, until it looks like hamburger ground. Place meat in a large dishpan with salt, sage, and crushed red pepper. Put on disposable gloves. Take your hands and mix these ingredients until they are mixed evenly throughout the ground meat. Makes 5 to 7 patties.

Don't sit on this recipe. What I mean is: don't take the measurements for seasoning I gave you as the gospel truth. If I were in your kitchen, it would be different. But I can't see the meat you're mixing. You are the one who has to perfect this recipe. It merely takes ingenuity.

The Ingenuity Test: Dip up a patty and fry it in a skillet. Taste for salt. Is it enough, or do you wish to add some more? Does it have enough sage? Once seasonings are all right, divide sausage into one-pound freezer bags, put into freezer, and use as needed.

Mama says never put a raw rib on the grill before barbecuing. The ribs must be "jecked" first. "Jecking" is slang pronunciation in the black culture for "jerking," which, in this case, means boiling.

For seasoning salt, use your favorite store-bought brand.

Barbecued Spare Ribs

2 slabs marinated ribs
1½ T. salt
2 T. pepper
1 T. seasoning salt
4 quarts water
1 cup celery, chopped
1 cup bell pepper, chopped
2 large onions, chopped

Overnight, marinate ribs on each side with salt, pepper, and seasoning salt. Cover and refrigerate until morning. In a deep boiler add water, marinated ribs, celery, bell pepper and onions. Boil for 90 minutes. Place ribs on grill, braising or browning them slowly and evenly on each side. Dip ribs in Uncle Sam's Bar-B-Que Sauce (next page) or your own favorite sauce. Serves 3 or 4.

Uncle Sam's Bar-B-Que Sauce

The smoke-flavored sauce used is generally Old Hickory Smoking Sauce, which is a liquid smoke.

2 quarts water
3 lemons, chopped, rind and juice
2 onions, chopped
2 cups celery, chopped fine
2 bell peppers, chopped
3 bay leaves
1 can tomato paste
2 bottles tomato catsup (16-ounce size)
3-ounce jar mustard
4 T. chili powder
¼ cup barbecue powder, mesquite
2 T. smoke-flavored sauce
1 stick butter
¾ cup sugar
½ cup ribbon cane syrup
1 T. crushed red pepper
1 tsp. hot sauce
¼ cup vinegar
1 T. salt
1 tsp. pepper

Use a deep boiler to mix ingredients. Add water, lemons, onions, bell pepper, celery, and bay leaves. Boil for 25 minutes. Add tomato paste, catsup, mustard, chili powder, mesquite, smoke-flavored sauce, butter, sugar, syrup, red pepper, hot sauce, vinegar, salt, and pepper. Simmer for 2 to 2½ hours until thick. Brush on favorite meats. Yield: about 1 gallon.

Pig Tails and Pig Ears, Southern Style

2 pounds pig tails
1 pound pig ears
2 tsp. salt
2 tsp. pepper
3½ quarts water
1 tsp. crushed red pepper
2 slices lemon

Wash pig tails and pig ears. Season with salt and pepper. Add pig tails and pig ears to water and put in the crushed red pepper and lemon slices. Simmer uncovered for 4 hours and serve. Yields 5 to 6 servings.

Pork Chops and Gravy

6 center-cut pork chops
2 cups flour
2 tsp. salt
1½ tsp. pepper
4 cups oil
1 sliced onion
3 cups water

Mix flour with salt and pepper. Take each pork chop and dip in water. Dredge with flour until covered completely. Place in cast-iron skillet of preheated oil, and cook on medium heat until golden brown. After all pork chops are golden brown, pour all oil from skillet, except ¼ cup. Place pork chops back in skillet with onions. Add water and simmer until gravy is thick.
Serves 3.

Beef

Beef and Noodles

2 pounds beef stew meat
2 tsp. salt
1 tsp. seasoning salt
1 tsp. pepper
1 5-ounce bag of noodles
1 cup chopped onions
1 cup chopped bell peppers

In a boiler ¾ filled with water, add beef, salt, seasoning salt, pepper, onions, and bell peppers. Simmer on low heat for 2 hours. Add noodles to beef stew and stock. Cook for 30 minutes on low heat, stirring constantly. Serve with corn bread. Serves 8 to 10.

Stewed Beef in Onions

    2 pounds beef stew meat
    2 tsp. meat tenderizer (optional)
    2 tsp. salt
    1 tsp. seasoning salt
    2 tsp. pepper
    2 sliced onions
    ½ cup plain flour, sifted
    2 pints water

Season stew meat in boiler with meat tenderizer, salt, seasoning salt, pepper and onions. Add water. Cook for 90 minutes on medium heat. Make thickening and add. Continue to cook for 20 to 30 minutes more, until simmered to a gravy. Serves 8 to 10.

Thickening

Add 1½ cups of cool water to ½ cup flour, mixing until lumps have disappeared. Then pour into skillet and simmer until gravy is thick.

Broiled Liver and Onions

8 slices baby calf (beef) liver
1 T. salt
2 tsp. pepper
1 cup vegetable oil
2 onions, sliced
¾ cup plain white flour
1 quart water

Season liver on both sides with salt and pepper. Place liver in slightly warmed skillet, frying in oil until browned. Add onions and flour, stir-frying for 5 minutes. Pour water into skillet, and simmer liver for 60 minutes or until tender. Serves 4 to 5.

Grilled Steak

5 ¾-inch T-bone steaks
2 tsp. salt
l tsp. seasoning salt
2 tsp. pepper

Spread salt, pepper and seasoning salt evenly on each side of steak. In a bread pan, slide steak into grill section of oven, browning at 375 degrees to desired doneness on each side. Serve with baked potato and green salad. Serves 5.

Pepper Steak

20 pieces sirloin, cut in thin strips (about ½"
    thick and 3" to 4" long)
2 tsp. salt
2 tsp. pepper
⅛ tsp. oil
½ cup plain white flour
2 cups bell pepper (in strips)
1 cup onions (in strips)
3 cups water

Cover sirloin pieces with salt and pepper. In skillet, preheat oil, browning sirloin strips evenly. Sprinkle flour on sirloin, adding bell pepper and onions. Pour water on sirloin for simmering. Simmer in skillet for 60 minutes or until tender. Serve over rice. Serves 5 to 6.

Round Steak Deluxe

2 round steak portions
2 T. meat tenderizer (optional)
2 tsp. salt
2 tsp. pepper
2 onions, chopped

Before the days of meat tenderizer, if you wanted to tenderize meat, you pounded it with a wooden mallet or the edge of a saucer.

25

1 cup bell pepper, chopped

2 cups water

1 cup onions, chopped (optional)

Combine meat tenderizer, salt and pepper and sprinkle evenly over both sides of meat. Brown both sides of meat. Add onions and bell peppers and stir-fry. Add thickening and simmer for 60 minutes. About 15 minutes before completion of cooking, add cup of chopped onions, if desired. Serves 5 to 6.

Stovetop Roast Beef

4 T. vegetable oil

3 pounds roast beef

1 tsp. salt (more if desired)

1 tsp. seasoning salt, optional

2 tsp. pepper

1 cup water

2 cups onions, sliced

½ cup plain white flour

Preheat oil in a double boiler or skillet. Sprinkle roast with salt, pepper and seasoning salt. Brown roast on each side in skillet. Add water and simmer for 2 hours, then add onions and thickening. Simmer for 30 minutes.

Meatloaf

3 pounds ground chuck
2 onions, chopped finely
1 cup bell pepper, chopped finely
2 cans tomato paste (6 ounce)
½ cup plain white flour
1½ tsp. salt
½ tsp. pepper
2 eggs
1 quart water

When I was growing up, we generally ate meatloaf when we were tired of spaghetti and hamburgers. In my house meatloaf is still a special dish.

Place ground chuck in a large bowl, and mix in onions, bell peppers, 1 can of tomato paste, flour, salt, pepper, and eggs. Form mixture into a loaf. Spread remaining can of tomato paste over top of loaf. Put in a large bread pan and cover with foil, adding 1 quart of water to loaf pan, and bake at 375 degrees. Serves 8 to 10.

Stuffed Bell Pepper

6 medium-sized bell peppers
2 pounds ground beef
2 tsp. salt
1 tsp. pepper
1 cup chopped onions
½ cup plain white flour
2 eggs
1 small can tomato paste
1 cup water

Place ground beef in a large bowl, and add salt, pepper, onions, tomato paste, eggs and flour. Mix ingredients well. Hull out insides of bell pepper (seeds and pulpy matter), leaving bottom intact. Stuff meat mixture into bell peppers. Place stuffed peppers in roasting pan, and cover bottom of pan with water. Bake for 1 hour at 375 degrees. Serves 6.

Hot Tamales

Cornmeal mixture

2 cups plain cornmeal
¾ cup milk
2 tsp. salt
1 egg, beaten

Beef mixture

1 pound beef (portion of round steak, chuck roast, or other cut)
1½ quarts water
3 tsp. salt
½ tsp. garlic salt

Sauce

1 six-ounce can tomato paste
2 cups water
½ cup hot sauce (Louisiana brand or similar)
⅛ cup olive oil

Wrappers

12 large dried corn shucks (these may be bought, packaged, in grocery store)
string

1. In a bowl, mix cornmeal, milk, salt, and egg to form a batter. Place this mixture in the refrigerator and allow it to cool until meat is ready.

My grandmama's sister Minnie had a cafe back in 1927, and hot tamales and barbeque were the main dishes she served. Minnie taught Grandma how to make hot tamales. How Minnie learned I don't know.

Nearly every Delta town has a hot tamale stand.

2. Cook beef in water with salt and garlic salt added. Simmer over medium heat until so tender the meat falls apart—2 or 3 hours.

3. In a bowl mix tomato paste, water, hot sauce, and olive oil. Stir until mixed well.

4. Soak corn shucks in warm water for about an hour so they will be pliable.

5. On a clean table top, spread out cornshucks and spread cornmeal batter onto each shuck, leaving about 1″ at each end. Place 1 tablespoon of shredded beef down the center of the batter. Then cover with another layer of batter and add one tablespoon of the sauce on top. Roll the shucks closed from the sides and close each end by folding the shuck down. Continue procedure until all shucks are filled.

6. Tie 3 tamales together with string and place 4 groups of tamales onto a baking sheet (one not too deep but with a one to one and one-half inch rim). Pour remaining sauce over the tamales and bake in the oven at 375 degrees for about 45 to 55 minutes. Serve hot. Yields 3 or 4 servings.

Soups, Stews, and Such

Egg Drop Soup

    3 cups chicken broth
    2 eggs, beaten
    ½ tsp. salt
    ½ cup chopped green onion tops

In a boiler, bring chicken broth to a hard boil. Add eggs and salt, stirring briskly. Sprinkle in onions after soup has boiled for 5 minutes. Serve hot. Serves 4 persons.

This recipe for egg drop soup was learned from a Chinese friend of my grandmama's who ran a grocery in Hollandale. There are a lot of groceries run by Chinese in the Delta.

After Easter, most black families didn't eat stews and soups and chitterings, because they felt putting really hot food in your stomach in hot weather would cause food to "sour in your stomach." They mostly ate stews and soups in cold weather.

See page 117 for homemade vegetable mix for soups. Or add butter beans, okra, tomatoes and other vegetables fresh from the garden.

Chicken Noodle Soup

2 fryers or 2 medium hens
1 5-ounce bag of egg noodles (medium size)
3 quarts water, more if needed
1 stick butter
1 T. salt
2 tsp. pepper
2 tsp. herb seasoning, optional

Cut fryer or hen into portions. Place in deep boiler of water. Add butter, salt, pepper and herb seasoning. Simmer until tender. Remember: cooking time will vary for a fryer and a hen. A fryer will be done in 45 to 60 minutes, but a hen will take 2 hours. Test your bird with a fork. When the meat is tender, proceed to add noodles and cook in the chicken stock for 20 to 30 minutes. Add more water to stock if desired. Serve with favorite bread and salad. Serves 8 to 10.

Hock Bone Soup

4 to 5 medium ham hock bones
4 quarts water
2 #303 cans whole kernel corn
1 T. salt (more, if desired)

2 bags frozen mixed vegetables (home-frozen
   or bought)
2 cans tomato paste (4-ounce cans)
1 tsp. pepper
1 tsp. butter or margarine

Place hock bones in water and cook for 2 hours,
partially covered, on medium heat, on top of stove.
Add corn, salt, mixed vegetables, tomato paste, pepper and butter. Cook for 45 minutes on medium
heat, partially covered. Serves 10 to 12 persons.

Blue Monday Soup
Southern Style Vegetable Soup

4 quarts water
2 pounds stew meat or cut-up roast
3 tsp. salt
l tsp. pepper
32-ounce frozen bag of mixed vegetables OR
   2 16-ounce cans vegetable mix
2 16-ounce cans whole kernel corn
2 6-ounce cans tomato paste
4 ears corn
1½ cups okra

My grandma had friends who knew she was always too busy to entertain, so they all decided they would start a club for themselves, and they called themselves the "Blue Monday Friends." Every Monday morning, no matter if it rained or snowed, they met up at Grandma's Fair Deal Cafe. The menu would always be homemade soup, corn bread and all of the liquor they could get on the table. And they would sit around and drink until Monday night. There was only one thing I never understood: my grandma would drink as much as everybody, but never would get drunk.

Put water, stew meat, salt, and pepper into a boiler and simmer for 2 hours. Then add vegetable mix, kernel corn and tomato paste. Simmer for 45 minutes. In the last 15 minutes of simmering, add okra and corn on the cob, each ear cut into 2 or 3 pieces. Serves 10 to 12 persons.

Homemade Beef Stew

3 pounds beef stew meat
3 quarts water
2 tsp. salt
1 tsp. pepper
2 tsp. seasoning salt
4 potatoes, cubed
4 carrots, cubed
1 #303 can whole tomatoes, cut up

Thickening:
1 cup plain white flour
3 cups water

In a boiler, place stew meat in 3 quarts of water, adding salt, pepper and seasoning salt. Boil for 90 minutes. Drain meat. In a large skillet, add stew meat, potatoes, carrots and tomatoes. Add thickening, stirring in well. Cover and simmer for 60 minutes. Serve over rice. Yields 6 to 8 servings.

Chicken and Shrimp Gumbo

4 slices salt pork

4 quarts water

2 fryer's portions, cooked with all bones removed

1 16-ounce can whole kernel corn

2 cups mixed vegetables

2 tsp. Worcestershire sauce

3 bay leaves

2 16-ounce cans whole tomatoes

1 6-ounce can tomato sauce

salt, as desired

½ tsp. pepper

½ cup thickening (see below)

2 cups okra, cut up

24 medium shrimp, deveined

We used to go to the trouble of browning thickening, or making a roux, but we don't do that anymore because it takes too long and really isn't necessary.

Boil salt pork for 25 minutes in water. Add chicken portions and cook for 60 minutes on medium heat, adding corn, vegetables, Worcestershire sauce, bay leaves, tomatoes, tomato sauce, salt and pepper. Then add okra and shrimp and ½ cup of thickening (1½ cups of water and ¾ cup of flour). Simmer for 30 minutes. Serves 10 to 12.

Homemade Chili and Beans

3 quarts water
4 strips bacon or salt pork
2 T. vegetable shortening
1 pound bag of pinto or red beans
3 tsp. salt
1 tsp. pepper
1 tsp. vegetable oil
3 pounds ground chuck
4 T. chili powder or chili mix
2 onions, chopped
2 bell peppers, chopped
½ cup Worcestershire sauce
1 6-ounce can tomato sauce
1 6-ounce can tomato paste
1 tsp. mustard
1 cup barbecue sauce

In a boiler, add salt pork and water, cooking for 30 minutes. Soak beans in warm water while salt pork is cooking. Add beans, shortening, 1 teaspoon salt, and pepper. Cook for 2 hours. In a cast-iron skillet, stir-fry with oil the ground chuck, chili mix, onions, and bell pepper. Add Worcestershire sauce, two teaspoons salt, tomato sauce, tomato paste, mustard, and barbecue sauce. Pour ground beef mixture into beans and simmer for 30 to 45 minutes. Serves 10 to 15.

Neckbone and Macaroni Stew

3 pounds neckbones
3½ quarts water
1 T. salt
1 tsp. pepper
1 bag of macaroni (8-ounce bag of elbow macaroni)
2 6-ounce cans tomato paste

In deep boiler, add water and neckbones seasoned with salt and pepper. Simmer for 2 hours. When neckbones are tender, add macaroni and tomato paste. Simmer for another 30 minutes. Serve hot with corn bread. Serves 8 to 10.

Sausage, Red Beans and Rice

1 pound red kidney beans
3 quarts water
5 strips salt pork
⅓ cup vegetable shortening
1 tsp. salt
1 tsp. sugar

This is known as "The Poor Man's Dinner."

Hunger was something that the black family had to conquer, and it was a must that simple foods be designed to bring out a delicious meal. My grandma, even today, can tell you stories of how proud she felt about her sister, Malinda, who could walk up from the cotton field and find company sitting on her steps, and she would take a shelf of nothing and make the best meal you ever tasted.

3 bay leaves
⅛ cup vegetable oil
2 to 3 pounds smoked sausage
2 onions, chopped
2 bell peppers, chopped
3 T. herb seasoning mix

Soak beans in warm water for 30 to 40 minutes, or overnight, as desired. Drain excess water from beans after they have soaked. In a separate boiler, boil salt pork and water for 45 minutes. Drain and add fresh water to salt pork, simmering for 20 minutes. Now add beans, shortening, salt, sugar, and bay leaves, and simmer on stove top for 2 hours, stirring occasionally.

In a separate boiler, boil smoked sausage for 15 to 20 minutes. Remove sausage from water and cut into bite-size pieces. In a skillet place oil, bell peppers, onions, and herb seasoning mixture. Add sausage and cook mixture for 12 minutes, stirring as it cooks. Once slightly browned, the mixture is poured into the beans, stirred, and cooked for 20 to 30 minutes. Serve over steamed rice. (See recipe on page 114.)

Spaghetti and Franks

1 box spaghetti (7-ounce box, extra long)
4 quarts water
3 tsp. salt, more if desired
⅓ cup oil
1 cup celery, chopped
2 medium onions, chopped
1 cup bell pepper, chopped
2 6-ounce cans tomato paste
10 wieners/franks, chunked (1″ thick pieces)
1 tsp. pepper

Place spaghetti in 3 quarts of boiling water with 1 teaspoon salt, and boil for 15 to 20 minutes. Drain spaghetti. Place oil in skillet and preheat. Brown onions, bell pepper and celery. Add tomato paste, 1 quart of water, and remaining salt and pepper. Simmer for 15 minutes. Add franks and cook for 15 minutes longer. Pour sauce over spaghetti. Serves 6 to 8.

Spaghetti and Meat Sauce

1 7-ounce box of spaghetti, extra long
4 quarts water
3 tsp. salt
1 tsp. vegetable oil
3 pounds hamburger chuck, ground
1 tsp. pepper
1 tsp. seasoning salt
2 medium onions, chopped
2 cups bell pepper, chopped
2 6-ounce cans tomato paste

Place spaghetti in 3 quarts of boiling water with 1 teaspoon salt, and boil for 15 to 20 minutes. Drain spaghetti.

Meat Sauce: In a skillet, add oil, warming slightly. In a bowl, mix ground beef, 2 teaspoons salt, pepper, and seasoning salt. Add to skillet and brown; then add onions and bell peppers. Simmer for 10 to 15 minutes. Add tomato paste and 1 quart of water, and stir until mixed well. Simmer for 25 to 30 minutes or until tender. Pour mixture over drained spaghetti. Yields 5 to 7 servings.

Tomato Meat Sauce, No. 2

2 tsp. vegetable oil
3 pounds ground beef
2 T. salt
1 T. pepper
1 cup bell peppers, chopped
1 cup onions, chopped
½ clove garlic, chopped
½ cup celery, chopped
2 6-ounce cans tomato paste
¼ cup Worcestershire sauce
1½ quarts water

Add oil to a large cast-iron skillet, crumble beef and cook until brown. Add salt, pepper, bell peppers, onions, garlic, celery, tomato paste, Worcestershire sauce, and water. Stir constantly until thick and saucy.

Wild Game

We always called all birds, even quail and dove, wild birds, just like we call all berries, wild berries, even after we found out they were dewberries or blackberries.

Fried Wild Birds

2 wild birds
2 cups plain flour
1½ cups vegetable oil
1 T. salt
1½ tsp. pepper
3 cups water

Cut up birds into frying parts just like chickens—right down the middle. Wash well. Warm oil in a skillet. Take flour, salt and pepper to form a shaking bag. Put birds in bag and flour evenly. Place in skillet and brown on each side over medium heat. Add water. Smother until tender, about 60 minutes. Serve bird and gravy over rice.

Oven-Baked Coon with Yams

1 coon, demusked
2½ T. salt
1 T. pepper
2 tsp. crushed red pepper
5 sweet potatoes, medium
¾ cup sugar, more if desired
1 stick butter
2½ quarts water, more or less as desired
1 small onion
lemon slices

When you decide to prepare coon, check for "musk" in the sweat glands. These are small grains of fat attached to the skin. They will change the aroma and the flavor of the coon if not removed. Boil coon in separate water for 2 hours to remove wildness. Drain and put in roasting pan. Take salt and pepper and rub all over the inside and outside of the coon. Sprinkle with crushed red pepper. Stuff onion into the chest. Add water and place whole peeled sweet potatoes around the coon. Sprinkle sweet potatoes with sugar and butter and top with lemon slices. Cover with foil. Cook at 350 degrees for 90 minutes until tender. Serves 6 to 8.

Coon and sweet potatoes and mustard greens make a great combination.

Every once in a while, a hunting friend will bring me a coon. He will be skinned and demusked before I get him, but still I have to check carefully under the arms and around the legs. The musk on a coon must be removed or you are in trouble. You look along the thighs and around the shoulder, the neck and the backbone. It resembles a hard whitish fat substance along the sweat glands of the coon's body.

43

Some people might put coon and possum in the same category, but I certainly don't. A coon baked with sweet potatoes is delicious, but I won't touch a possum. Traditionally black families will not eat possum because of the old saying that possums are grave robbers (they dig up people from graves and eat them). Even though I know it probably isn't true, I still can't get it out of my head, and so, for that reason, I don't eat possum today.

Barbecued Deer Ribs

5 pounds deer ribs
3½ quarts water
2 T. salt, more if desired
1 T. pepper
2 cups onions, chopped
1 cup celery, chopped
3 T. meat tenderizer

Marinate ribs overnight in ½ gallon vinegar and 3 tablespoons salt, turning several times. The next morning, add water to marinade, and cook on stove top for 2 hours on medium heat. Remove water from pan. Boil ribs in new water to cover for 1½ hours, adding salt, pepper, onions, celery, and meat tenderizer. Remove from boiler, straining away all juices, and leaving onions and celery on top of venison. Place on barbecue grill, and grill until browned evenly and tender. Brush on barbecue sauce and grill for 45 minutes. See page 19 for Uncle Sam's Bar-B-Que Sauce. Serves 8 to 10.

Deer Stew

2 slabs ribs or meat cut up for stew
2 quarts water for each cooking time
1 quart vinegar
2 T. salt for each cooking time
2 cups Irish potatoes, sliced
2 cups onions, chopped
1 T. pepper
1 T. meat tenderizer
2 cups tomatoes, cut up
16-ounce can tomato paste
mixed vegetables, if desired

In a boiler, boil ribs or stew meat for 1½ hours in water, vinegar, and salt. Drain water from meat. Add deer ribs to new water, potatoes, onions, salt, pepper, and meat tenderizer. Simmer for 1½ hours on stove top. In final cooking stage, add tomatoes, mixed vegetables, and tomato paste, and simmer for an additional 30 minutes. Yields 10 to 12 servings.

Venison, considered to be an expensive delicacy in northern restaurants, is an everyday treat for black families. Hunting game is a sport among black men in the South.

Irish potatoes, in the South, means all potatoes except sweet potatoes. Sometimes we say red potatoes and white potatoes and Idaho bakers, but mostly we say Irish potatoes. Irish potatoes were named for the Irish because they were longtime potato growers.

You can use a bag of frozen vegetables, or a can of vegetables, with cut-up celery, onions, okra, potatoes, and carrots. Of course, fresh vegetables are great.

Venison is a tough
grain of meat. It takes
marinating for full
enjoyment.

Oven-Baked Deer Ham

1 deer ham, approximately 8 to 10 pounds
3 cups vinegar
2 cups onions, chopped
salt and pepper, as needed
1 cup bell peppers, chopped
2 cups celery, chopped
1½ cups ribbon cane syrup
4 slices pineapple and juice

Marinate deer ham overnight in 3 cups of vinegar
and salty water, turning several times. The next
morning, cook in same water for about 2 hours on
top of stove over high heat. Remove water and
cover ham evenly with salt and pepper. Put in
roasting pan and add water, onions, bell pepper and
celery. Bake for 3 hours at 350 degrees. Remove
from oven, cover with syrup, and dress up with
pineapple slices and juice. Brown for 20 minutes.
Serves 12 to 15 persons.

Rabbit Supreme

1 rabbit, cleaned and cut up
2 cups vinegar
¾ cup flour
2 T. salt
1 T. pepper
2 cups vegetable oil
1½ cups onion, chopped
2½ cups water

This is one of my favorite recipes. I named it Supreme because I thought it was special. Generally, one of my hunting friends brings me rabbits during rabbit season.

To cook rabbit, you want to wash it well. Then marinate in 2 cups of vinegar for 45 minutes. Take flour, salt, and pepper to form a shaking bag. Cut up rabbit, place it in the bag, and shake to cover evenly with flour. In skillet of warm oil, brown rabbit on both sides. Remove 1¾ cups of oil from skillet. Place chopped onion over rabbit. Add water and simmer over low heat for 1 to 1½ hours until tender. Serve over rice. Yields 3 to 4 servings. (This rabbit can also be smothered by just putting a lid over the skillet.)

I thought Squirrel Delight would be a good name for this recipe. because my family is always so delighted when I serve it.

Squirrel Delight

1 squirrel
¾ cup oil
½ cup flour
1½ T. salt
2 tsp. pepper
2 cups water

Wash and cut squirrel in portions. In a skillet, warm oil. Take flour, salt and pepper to form a shaking bag. Flour squirrel evenly. Fry and brown on both sides. Pour water into skillet and allow to simmer uncovered for 1 to 1½ hours until tender. Yields 3 to 4 servings.

Mixed Squirrel Sausage

3 squirrels, deboned
2 to 3 T. salt (taste for desired amount)
⅓ ounce sage
1 tsp. pepper
⅛ cup crushed red pepper
1 set disposable gloves

These squirrels must be washed thoroughly, and all meat should be trimmed from the squirrels;

make sure no bone is left in the meat. Grind meat finely for sausage. Put on gloves and mix in salt, sage, pepper, and red pepper until all ingredients have practically disappeared into the sausage. Make sausage into patties and fry in skillet with less than 1 teaspoon oil to keep from sticking. Freeze unused sausage in freezer bags. Yields 20 to 25 patties.

Venison Mixed Sausage

5 pounds deer meat, ground finely
5 T. salt
5 T. sage
1 tsp. pepper
2 tsp. crushed red pepper
1 set disposable gloves

Grind venison finely for sausage. With gloves on, add salt, sage, pepper and crushed red pepper. Mix well in dishpan. To try out for taste, make a patty and fry slowly in 1 tablespoon oil, browning evenly on both sides. Freeze unused sausage in freezer bags. Yields 25 or 30 servings.

To Skin a Turtle:

All turtles have hard backs. You'll need a sharp knife. Take the blade of a sharp knife, and cut the meat away from the turtle's shell. The feet can be skinned and cleaned and cooked along with the other turtle meat. The shell can be thoroughly dried out and later used as a flower pot. It makes a unique arrangement. Turtle shells were also used for watering troughs in the chicken yard.

Turtle Stew

1 turtle, cut up
2 T. salt
1 tsp. pepper
2 onions, chopped
1 can whole tomatoes, #303
2 cups celery, chopped
8 potato wedges
¾ stick butter
2 quarts water

Skin meat from turtle shell and wash. Cut up in 2″ cubes for boiling. Add salt, pepper, onions, tomatoes, and celery to meat of turtle. Add water and simmer for 2 hours. Add potatoes last, and continue to simmer for 30 minutes until tender. Yields stew for 8 to 10 persons.

SPRING

Poultry
Fish and Seafood
Eggs
Cheese
Sandwiches

S pring in the Delta is a beautiful time. In March farmers can get in the fields and start breaking up the land and plowing. They still use the old saying that when the pecan trees bud, you can plant corn, and when the pecan buds are as big as a squirrel's ear, you can plant cotton.

When I was a child, I used to love to go out in the fields and pastures, looking for wild greens and poke sallet, and sometimes wild onions and garlic. The onions and garlic were so strong, we didn't use them often. For Easter, we always had a nice ham, and we always had mustard greens.

Easter dinner

Baked Ham
Potato Salad
Mustard Greens
Candied Sweet Potatoes
Yeast Rolls
Corn bread
Coconut Cake
Pecan Pie
Iced Tea

Spring was fishing time too, and early in the morning or late in the afternoon, we'd go down to the creek bank, and throw in our lines. If it was still too chilly to sit on the ground, we'd turn our bait buckets upside down and sit on them. It was nice to come home with a string of white perch and breams to change the winter diet, and sometimes a big turtle for soup.

Gardens were planted early so the vegetables would come in as soon as possible. Blackberries and dewberries would begin to ripen all along the railroad track. (When I was a kid, we always called them wild berries, just like we called all birds, like quail and doves, wild birds.) My grandmama says if you were riding the Bigleben train from Hollandale to Leland, sometimes the conductor would let you off to pick a hat full of berries, while the train was stopped at some little station. Back in the old days at my great-grandfather Fleming's, when spring came they'd still have hams in the smokehouse, sweet potatoes in the "sweet potato pump," corn in the corn crib (the little shed to store corn for the horses, cows and chickens), and fresh ground meal. But everyone was waiting for the little chickens to become broilers and the English peas and butter beans to be ready for the table.

Poultry

Boiled Chicken Feet and Legs

4 to 8 chicken feet
1 pot scalding water
1 quart water
2 tsp. salt
2 tsp. pepper
2 T. butter

In a pan, add chicken feet and scalding water to remove skin from the feet. Peel skin off completely. Now they're ready to cook. In a boiler, cook feet, adding water, salt, pepper and butter. Simmer for 1 hour over medium heat, or until tender. Serve over rice. Serves 2 to 4 persons.

Fried Chicken Feet and Legs

4 to 8 chicken feet
1 pot scalding hot water
2 cups plain flour
2 tsp. salt, more if desired
2 tsp. pepper, more if desired
½ quart vegetable oil

In a pan, pour scalding water over chicken feet to remove skin. Peel skin completely off. Warm oil in skillet. In a bag, add flour, salt, and pepper, shaking to mix well. Add feet to mixture, covering completely. Place feet and legs into warmed oil, and fry to a golden brown. You may make a gravy and serve with rice. Serves 2 to 4 persons.

Oven-Baked Barbecued Chicken

2 whole fryers, split
2 tsp. salt
2 tsp. pepper
½ tsp. paprika
½ cup onions, chopped
½ cup bell pepper, chopped
2 cups water

Don't think parents were cruel giving the children chicken feet and legs when the preacher came to visit: that was what they often got, whether the preacher visited or not. Strange as it may seem, they really tasted good.

Place fryer in roasting pan. Sprinkle evenly with salt, pepper, and paprika, adding onions, bell pepper, and water. Bake in oven for 45 minutes at 375 degrees. Remove and cover generously with barbecue sauce (recipe below).

Barbecue Sauce

1 quart of your favorite barbecue sauce
¼ cup gin or vodka
½ stick butter
3 tsp. sugar, plain
½ cup brown sugar
¾ cup syrup
½ cup mustard
¼ cup Worcestershire sauce

Place boiler over heat. Add sauce, butter, plain and brown sugar, syrup, vodka, mustard and Worcestershire sauce. Cook for 10 to 15 minutes. Spread over oven-baked chicken and barbecue in oven for 30 minutes. Serves 5 or 6 persons.

Chicken and Candied Wing Sauce

3 pounds chicken wings
4 cups flour, plain white
4 tsp. salt
3 tsp. pepper
seasoning salt
5 cups vegetable oil

In a shake bag, mix flour, salt and pepper. Put wings in bag, and shake until they are evenly covered. Warm oil in a deep skillet, and fry a golden brown. Serves 10 persons.

Candied Wing Sauce

2 cups ribbon cane syrup
½ cup hot sauce (bought kind, such as Louisiana Hot Sauce)
¾ stick butter

Use a Pyrex dish that can be put on top of stove. Mix in syrup, butter, and hot sauce, stirring and cooking until bubbly, about 8 to 10 minutes. Dip wings into sauce and serve.

Chicken and Dumplings

1 3-pound hen
2½ tsp. salt
1½ tsp. pepper
3 quarts water
¾ stick butter

Cut hen into portions. Place in a deep boiler with 3 quarts of water. Add salt, pepper, and butter. Simmer for 90 minutes. Add dumplings and cook for 30 minutes until tender. Serves 10 to 12.

Dumplings

3 cups flour, plain
3 eggs
½ tsp. salt
¼ cup cool water

In a large bowl, mix together flour, eggs, salt, and water, until dough forms. Set dough aside for 1 hour until settled. Roll dough out onto floured kneading board, as thin as possible, and cut into 2″ long strips. Drop each dumpling singly into hen and stock and cook for 30 minutes. Serve with favorite salad.

Country Style Baked Hen

1 3-pound hen
2 tsp. salt
½ tsp. pepper
2 onions, chopped
2 cups celery, chopped
¼ cup bell pepper, chopped
¾ stick butter

Place hen on cutting board and sprinkle evenly with salt and pepper. Put hen into a deep roasting pan filled halfway with water. Add onions, celery, bell pepper and butter. Place in oven and bake for 2½ hours at 375 degrees. Serves 6 to 8.

Miz Augustine's Oven-Baked Chicken

2 fryers, split
2 tsp. salt
1 tsp. seasoning salt
1 onion, chopped
1 cup celery, chopped
½ stick butter
1 quart water

Sam Chatmon at Fair Deal Cafe

Many famous persons have had dinner at my grandmama's cafe, including local blues singers such as Howlin' Wolf, B. B. King and Sam Chatmon. Mr. Sam was a regular, and he and his wife, Miz Augustine, were good friends of my grandmama's. Mr. Chatmon worked between tours at the compress in Hollandale, and during his season working in Hollandale, he spent his noon lunch hour eating at my grandmama's cafe on Blue Front. He would get his dinner, as we called it, and take Miz Augustine her dinner also. During my childhood and before, in the South, noon meals were called "dinner," and the

6:00 p.m. meal was called "supper." Sometimes Mr. Sam would come by the cafe and bring his guitar and play some of his blues hit recordings, while my grandmama would get his dinner prepared. He loved greens and fish. His wife, Miz Augustine, was also a good cook. Her recipe for chicken is the best baked chicken I've ever eaten.

This dressing can also be used as stuffing for pork roast.

Thickening

> 2 cups cool water
> ¾ cup plain white flour

Split chicken in half. Sprinkle salt, pepper, and seasoning salt evenly on both sides. Put in roasting pan, and add onion, celery, butter, and water. Cook for 90 minutes at 375 degrees. Remove from oven and add thickening. Cook for 25 minutes. Serve over rice or potatoes. Serves 5.

Dressing

> 1 oblong 10 x 12 inch pan of corn bread (2 days old)
> 10 slices plain white bread
> 3 eggs
> 4 T. sage
> 1 tsp. salt
> ½ tsp. pepper
> 2½ quarts chicken broth cooked with:
>> 2 cups onions
>> 2 cups celery
>> ½ stick butter

Crumble corn bread until all lumps are gone. Place in bowl, adding white bread and eggs. Pour broth with onions and celery directly onto bread, mashing bread into corn bread. Stir in sage, butter, salt, pepper, and more broth until all ingredients are mixed in well. The dressing should be well mixed in broth, so as not to dry. Bake in oven for 90 minutes at 350 degrees. Can serve 20 to 22. This dressing can be used as stuffing for any fowl or for pork roast.

Homemade Chicken Pot Pie

    2 pounds chicken breasts
    2½ quarts water
    2 tsp. salt
    1 tsp. pepper
    ½ tsp. seasoning salt
    ¾ stick butter
    1 bag frozen vegetable mix
    1 6-ounce can tomato sauce
    1 16-ounce can kernel corn

Thickening:
    ½ cup plain white flour
    ¾ cup water

Place breasts in deep boiler, with 2½ quarts of water, adding salt, pepper, seasoning salt, and butter. Simmer until tender for 60 minutes. Add vegetable mix, tomato sauce, kernel corn, and thickening. Simmer for 30 minutes until tender. Use Crust

Don't cook fried chicken too fast.

Recipe on page 168 for this pot pie. Cover the pan with crust. Pour in chicken and ingredients, draining off excess stock. Put crust over chicken to cover, making fork indentations. Bake crust at 350 degrees until brown (3 to 5 minutes). Serves 5 to 6.

Southern Fried Chicken

1 fryer, cut up
seasoning salt
3 cups plain white flour
3 tsp. salt
3 tsp. pepper
6 cups vegetable oil for deep frying

Cut fryer into portions. Sprinkle both sides evenly with seasoning salt. Put flour, salt and pepper in a paper bag and shake. Add chicken portions to bag and shake until they are completely covered. Use vegetable oil for frying in a deep skillet. Bring oil to a high warm state and place chicken in the skillet. Turn chicken as each side browns, until all pieces are completely brown.

Stovetop Chicken and Gravy

1 fryer, cut up in portions
3 cups plain white flour
2½ T. salt
1½ T. pepper
seasoning salt
6 cups vegetable oil
3 cups water

Some cooks call this Chicken Fricassee, but I like Stovetop Chicken and Gravy, because it tells you exactly what it is.

In a shaking bag, add flour, salt and pepper. Sprinkle seasoning salt evenly over chicken portions. Put chicken pieces in shaking bag and shake until covered evenly. In a deep skillet, add oil, and warm. Fry chicken until golden brown on each side, or until done. Remove all chicken from skillet. Pour out all oil into separate container to save, except for ¼ cup of oil. Place ½ cup of the chicken flour in the oil and brown, stirring constantly for 30 seconds. Pour in 3 cups of water to form gravy. Add chicken to gravy and cover, simmering for 10 to 15 minutes. Serve over rice. Serves 4 to 5.

This is one of my
own recipes, adapted
from my grandmama's
baked hen recipe.

Cornish Hen Supreme

4 Cornish hens
2 tsp. salt
2 tsp. pepper
1 stick butter
2 cups celery, chopped
2 cups onions, chopped
3 quarts water
4 bay leaves
4 oranges, peeled and quartered

Sprinkle salt and pepper over each Cornish hen. Into the chest of each hen, stuff ¼ stick of butter, celery and onions. Put in deep boiler with water. Place remaining butter, celery, and onions around the hens. Cover with foil and bake for 90 minutes at 375 degrees. Remove from oven and re-stuff each hen with 1 bay leaf and 1 orange each. Baste with juices until golden brown on barbecue grill over charcoal. Serves 5 to 6 persons.

Orange Glazed Duck

1 5- to 6-pound duck
2½ large onions, chopped
½ whole onion

3 cups celery, chopped
2 celery stems
3 tsp. salt
2 tsp. pepper
2 small oranges
water

This recipe may be used for both wild and domestic duck.

Remove packaging and wash duck thoroughly. Place giblets, neck and liver in the roasting pan. Stuff the onion half in the chest of the duck, along with 2 celery stems. Place duck in roasting pan and sprinkle evenly with salt and pepper. Fill the pan with water until it meets above the wings of the duck. Cover the roasting pan completely and tightly with foil. Bake at 350 degrees for 3 hours. Remove broth from duck (save broth). Squeeze orange juices on top of duck and cook until golden brown. Serves 5 or 6.

Duck Dressing

3 quarts stale corn bread
10 slices white bread
2 drops garlic juice
duck broth, with onion and celery that was
  cooked in the duck juice
2 large eggs, beaten

The stock from this turkey is to be used for dressing and giblet gravy.

Ninety percent of the people who don't like turkey dislike it because it is a considerably dry meat. My grandma taught me if you cover the turkey three-fourths with water and stuff the chest with butter, celery, and onion, it'll never be dry again. It's true. Try it!

1 tsp. salt
3 T. sage

In a large pan, crumble corn bread and white bread, adding duck broth and mashing until smooth. Add garlic juice, eggs, salt and sage, mixing all ingredients carefully. Place dressing in a roaster pan and bake at 350 degrees for 1½, or until firm. Yields 10 to 12 servings.

Southern Baked Turkey

1 12- to 15-pound turkey
2 onions, chopped
1 whole onion
2 cups celery, chopped (with 2 whole stems)
1 stick butter
3 tsp. salt
1 tsp. pepper
3½ quarts water

Thaw turkey fully, removing neck, gizzard and liver. Wash all parts thoroughly. In a roasting pan, place turkey stuffed with whole onion, celery stems, and butter. Sprinkle with salt and pepper. Place chopped onions and chopped celery around turkey, adding water. Cover completely with foil and bake at 350 degrees for 3½ hours. Serves 25 to 30.

Giblet Gravy

4 cups broth from fowl cooked with:
½ cup onions, chopped
½ cup celery, chopped
2 to 3 giblets, sliced thin
⅛ tsp. salt
⅛ tsp. pepper, if desired
2 hard-boiled eggs, sliced

Thickening:
¾ cup flour, plain
1½ cups cool water

Boil broth, adding giblets, salt, pepper, eggs, and thickening until it forms a gravy. Yields ½ gallon.

Turkey Hash

6 cups turkey, chopped
2 T. vegetable oil
3 cups Irish potatoes, chopped
5 tsp. salt
2 tsp. pepper
1½ cups water

Debone turkey, chop to hash. Pour oil in a skillet. Add turkey, potatoes, salt and pepper. Stir-fry for 20 minutes. Add water and simmer for 25 minutes. Serves 4 or 5.

Don't throw that holiday turkey away.

The fancy of a holiday table is a big 20-pound or larger turkey on the table with his legs sticking up. After two or three meals of turkey over the holidays, you get tired of it, but who can afford to throw it away? Hash that turkey and it'll be a delight.

Fish and Seafood

Miz Bob's Buffalo Fish

3 pounds buffalo fish, preferably rib portions
4 cups white cornmeal
2½ T. salt
1 T. black pepper
6 cups vegetable oil for deep frying
seasoning salt

Sprinkle seasoning salt on both sides of fish portions. Use a bag for shaking meal, salt and pepper. Mix well. Put fish portions in meal mix and cover evenly. Put meal-covered fish in large skillet of heated oil and cook over medium heat until golden brown. Serve with Louisiana hot sauce. Serves 8 to 10.

This was the one special item on the Saturday night menu at Fair Deal Cafe.

My uncle Ira was the fish cleaner at Fair Deal. On Saturday morning the fishermen would bring up 150 to 200 pounds of buffalo or cat for the Saturday lunch and dinners. Uncle Ira was a good cook, too.

Delta Fried Catfish

3½ pounds catfish
4 cups plain white meal
3 T. salt
2 T. pepper
seasoning salt
6 cups vegetable oil

Put seasoning salt on each of the fish portions. Place seasoned fish in a bag containing meal, salt and pepper. Shake until catfish is completely covered. In a large skillet, warm the oil and fry fish until golden brown. Serve with favorite sauce. Serves 5 to 6.

Stuffed Catfish Filet

5 whole catfish filets (7 to 8 inches long)
2 T. oil
2¾ cups corn bread
2¼ cups chicken broth
3½ slices stale white bread
2 T. sage
1 tsp. salt

Another fish we sometimes had was grinner. You fry it just like catfish. But remember: you have got to eat grinner when it's hot. Once it gets cold, the texture becomes mushy and it isn't as tasty. When my grandma was a young lady, she and her brothers would fish at an old lake called Grinner's Lake, located about 14 miles outside of Hollandale. The grinner got its name from the ugly look on its face. Also known in the Delta as a cypress trout because it lurks around the roots of cypress trees, it is really a bowfin trout.

2 eggs
5 tsp. melted butter
paprika

Grease bottom of a bread pan with vegetable oil and place each filet separately into the pan, splitting from end to end. Stuff each filet and bake in 350 degree oven for 30 to 45 minutes. Sprinkle lightly on top with paprika.

Catfish Stuffing Mix

Crumble corn bread and white bread finely, adding broth, sage, salt, oil, eggs and melted butter. Mix well and stuff into fish filets.

Boiled Crawfish

20 to 25 crawfish
1 pod red pepper
1 T. salt
2 bay leaves
1 tsp. allspice
2 T. butter

Boil crawfish in hot water at medium-high heat, adding pepper, salt, bay leaves, allspice, and butter. Boil for 20 minutes. Serve hot with crackers. Serves 2 or 3 people.

Lemon Broiled Fish

5 slices 7-to-8-inch size filets of catfish
2 tsp. salt
1½ lemons, sliced
½ stick melted butter
2 tsp. paprika

In a cake pan, place filets and cover each with salt, sliced lemons and melted butter. Spread melted butter evenly over filets and sprinkle lightly with paprika. Cover with foil and bake at 375 degrees for 30 minutes.

In later years, I learned from my grandmama how to stuff the crawfish shells, just like we stuff lobsters. Grandmama spent a lot of time in New Orleans when she was young,. so she knew about Louisiana cooking of fish and seafood.

When I was a kid, lobsters were not available to us, but my grandma always went crawfish hunting along with her friends, so I learned to crawfish early. Back then, crawfish were lined up along the "grudge" ditches and fishing banks. ("Grudge" ditches were drainage ditches also known as dredge ditches). We kids would take an old syrup bucket and fill it up with crawfish. The crawfish were so sweet and succulent, we'd eat half of the claws' fingers before we'd ever get home. But when we got home, we'd start the water right away to boil and cook the crawfish.

The gar fish has its own unique flavor. Once gar gets cold, its texture will toughen, but it is always a delicacy if served hot. Unlike gaspergou (fish), gar is a sweet fish.

Gar Stew

6 pounds gar meat
2½ cups water
1½ onions, chopped
½ tsp. salt
pepper, if desired
1 can whole tomatoes
1 can tomato sauce
3 T. flour
4 T. butter or margarine
½ tsp. lemon juice

Place water in boiler and add gar fish. Cook for 60 minutes on medium heat. Add chopped onions, salt, pepper, tomato sauce, whole tomatoes, flour, butter and lemon juice. Then cook for 55 minutes on medium heat, until very tender. Serves 10 to 12.

Stuffed Crab

1 pound crabmeat or the meat from about 12 crabs
1 pound sausage
3 cups day-old corn bread (see page 142)
5 slices white bread
2 T. sage

2 eggs, beaten well

4 chicken bouillon cubes

2 cups celery, chopped

2 cups onion, chopped

2 tsp. salt

½ stick butter

1 quart water

12 crab shells or aluminum shell-like containers

3 cups vegetable oil

In a bowl add crabmeat, sausage, corn bread, eggs, white bread, and sage, mixing ingredients well. Broth: in a boiler filled with 1 quart water, add bouillon cubes, celery, onions, salt, and butter. Simmer for 45 minutes. After the broth is completely simmered, strain off the celery and onion and save the broth. Mix the celery and onions into bread and meat mixture alternately with the broth until the dressing is stiff enough to stuff into the shells. This will take only about ¼ of the broth. Stuff the dressing into 12 shells. Deep-fat fry the shells in oil until they are golden brown. Serve hot with favorite cocktail sauce. Serves 12.

Grandma had a friend she used to visit in New Orleans named Mattie Johnson, who taught her how to cook crabs. Mattie used a white bread dressing for stuffing the crab, but my grandmama used her own corn bread to make it taste better. The same goes for the stuffed lobster.

Although we couldn't get fresh lobsters locally, when frozen lobsters came into the grocery stores, it was a great treat to buy a lobster and stuff it with corn bread like we stuffed crawfish.

Stuffed Lobster

3 quarts water
5 lobster tails
1 bag crab boil
3 cups stale corn bread
4 slices stale white bread
3 to 4 cups chicken broth
2 T. sage
2 eggs
1 tsp. salt
5 tsp. butter
paprika

In a deep boiler, bring water to a boil. Add crab boil and lobster tails. In 5 minutes, remove crab boil bag. Allow lobster tails to boil for 25 minutes. Remove the lobster from the pot, cut it vertically, and place in greased pan. To make the lobster stuffing, you crumble corn bread finely along with white bread. Add chicken broth, butter, sage, eggs, and salt. Stuff the split lobster and bake uncovered at 350 degrees for 30 minutes or until firm. Sprinkle paprika on top if desired.

Delta Fried Oysters

12 medium oysters
2 cups plain white flour
1 T. salt
1 T. seasoning salt
1 tsp. pepper
¼ cup sweet milk
2 eggs, beaten
6 cups vegetable oil

Mix flour, salt, seasoning salt and pepper in one bowl. In another bowl, mix milk and eggs. Take each oyster and dip into egg mixture. Then roll in flour mixture. Repeat the procedure. In skillet, warm oil and fry battered oysters to a golden brown. Serve with cocktail sauce. See shrimp sauce, page 78.

Oyster Loaf

12 medium oysters
1 tsp. salt
½ tsp. paprika
1 tsp. seasoning salt
2 eggs, beaten

2 tsp. butter

2 bay leaves

1 tsp. Worcestershire sauce

1 full loaf of yeast bread (Use the yeast roll recipe on page 145)

In bowl, mix raw oysters, salt, seasoning salt, eggs, butter, bay leaves, and Worcestershire sauce. Cut off end of bread loaf, and scoop out inside. Stuff ingredients into the loaf and wrap in aluminum foil or use a loaf pan to bake oyster loaf after stuffing. Bake in oven for 20 minutes at 350 degrees.

Salmon Croquettes

2 15½-ounce cans salmon, drained

2 tsp. salt

1 tsp. pepper

1 cup onions, chopped

2 eggs, beaten

3 T. plain white flour

2 cups vegetable oil

2 cups cracker crumbs, rolled out and crushed fine

In a bowl, mix salmon, salt, pepper, onions, eggs, and flour. Mix all ingredients well and roll into thick patties. Coat patties with cracker crumbs. Place oil in skillet, warming slightly. Place salmon patties in skillet and brown evenly on both sides. Serve hot with buttered rice. Yields 8 to 10 croquettes.

Fried Shrimp

24 medium or large shrimp, deveined, but with
    tails on
4 cups vegetable oil
2 eggs
2 T. milk
2 cups plain flour
2 tsp. salt
½ tsp. seasoning salt

Mix flour, salt, and seasoning salt. Beat 2 eggs with a dash of salt, adding milk until mixed well. Dip each shrimp separately in egg mixture until covered. Then roll shrimp in flour mixture. Repeat procedure. Place in a preheated skillet with oil, fry in deep oil to a golden brown.

Shrimp Etouffée

¾ cup bacon fat
3 T. mixed sausage
2 bunches green onions, chopped
2 bell peppers, chopped
2 tsp. salt
¾ cup all-purpose flour
2 tsp. browning sauce
2 cups water
2 cups crabmeat
3 pounds shrimp, deveined
½ cup hot sauce (Louisiana brand or similar)
2 tsp. pepper
rice, cooked

In a skillet add bacon fat, sausage, green onions, and bell pepper, and stir-fry until all ingrcdients are mixed well. In a bowl mix crabmeat, shrimp, hot sauce and pepper and pour into skillet with the other ingredients. Cover and simmer for about 20 minutes over low heat. Serve over rice. Yields 12 servings.

Shrimp Sauce

This is great with all kinds of seafoods.

¼ cup hot sauce
½ cup tomato catsup
½ cup sweet pickle relish
½ tsp. salt
½ tsp. pepper
⅓ cup A-1 sauce
⅓ cup Worcestershire sauce
⅓ cup finely grated bell pepper, pureed
2 tsp. sugar
1 tsp. spices, herb seasoning

In a bowl, mix hot sauce, tomato catsup, relish, salt, pepper, A-1 sauce, Worcestershire sauce, bell pepper, sugar, and herb seasoning. Mix well, chill and serve.

Eggs

French Toast

2 slices white bread
2 eggs
⅛ tsp. salt
1 T. milk
1 cup vegetable oil

Mix eggs, salt, and milk, beating until fluffy. Dip each slice of bread in egg mixture, covering well. Place into oil and brown on each side. Serve on plate with best table syrup over top.

Stuffed Eggs

6 hard-boiled eggs
2 T. mayonnaise or salad dressing
dash of salt
1 tsp. sugar
3 T. sweet pickle relish
paprika

Cut eggs in oblong halves. Remove yolks and mash well until lumps disappear. Mix into yolks, mayonnaise, salt, sugar and relish. Stuff into each egg half. Sprinkle paprika lightly on top.

Ham and Egg Omelet

2¼″ thick, pre-cooked ham slices, chopped
3 eggs, beaten
½ tsp. salt
¼ tsp. black pepper
2 tsp. white milk
2 T. oil

Place eggs in bowl. Add salt, pepper, and milk and beat well. Heat oil in skillet and pour in egg mixture, allowing it to spread full round of skillet. Cook eggs on medium heat and allow them to brown lightly. Pour ham onto omelet round. Gently lift one side of omelet with a spatula and fold omelet in half.

Cheese

Cheese toast makes a nice snack for breakfast, when you get tired of regular breakfast food.

Cheese Toast

4 slices white bread
1 T. butter
4 slices American cheese

On a cookie sheet, spread out each slice of bread, brushing evenly with butter. Place slice of American cheese on buttered side of each. Bake at 350 degrees for 3 minutes or until cheese has melted. Serves 4 persons.

Creamy Style Grits

1¾ cups grits
3 cups water
⅛ tsp. salt
¼ stick butter
1 cup small chunks of cheese

In a boiler, bring water to a hard boil, slowly stirring as you pour grits into boiler. Stir and simmer until creamy. Add salt, cheese and butter. Serve hot. Serves 5 to 6.

Macaroni and Cheese

1 8-ounce bag of macaroni
3 quarts water
1 pound hoop or cheddar cheese, chopped
¾ cup evaporated milk
dash of pepper
1 tsp. salt
¾ stick of butter or ¼ cup oil
2 eggs

Boil macaroni in water with salt for 20 minutes or until tender. Drain macaroni and place in a baking dish, mixing in cheese, milk, pepper, salt, butter and eggs. Cover top with cheese. Bake in oven at 375 degrees for 10 to 15 minutes or until firm, browning top of cheese lightly. Serves 7 to 8.

Sandwiches

Flatdog Sandwich

2 slices bologna
$\frac{1}{8}$ tsp. vegetable oil
2 slices white or wheat bread
1 tsp. mayonnaise
$\frac{1}{2}$ tsp. mustard

In a skillet, put oil, warming bologna on both sides. Spread mayonnaise and mustard easily on inside of bread. Place bologna on both sides of bread, and put together as a sandwich.

This was the most popular sandwich sold at Blue Front cafes in the 30's. This Flatdog Sandwich was sold for 15 cents and was considered the poor man's sandwich. My grandmama sold these anytime during the week.

These are the standards of a good hamburger on Blue Front and at home, when you talk about "having a hamburger."

Delta Cheeseburger

2 pounds ground beef
1 tsp. salt
1 tsp. seasoning salt
1 tsp. pepper
2 eggs
6 hamburger buns
2 T. butter or margarine
¼ cup mustard
6 slices cheese
6 slices tomatoes
6 slices onions
18 slices sweet pickles
½ cup mayonnaise
1 tsp. vegetable oil

In a large bowl, mix ground beef, salt, seasoning salt, pepper, and eggs, making 6 four-inch round hamburger patties. Grease skillet with vegetable oil, and fry each patty slowly until browned on each side. Take hamburger buns and spread each side with butter and brown lightly on each side in the oven. Remove and cover thinnest half of bun with mustard. Put hamburger patty on mustard side of bun. Put cheese on patty, and put in oven for 30 seconds. On top of cheese add tomatoes, onions and pickles. Spread left-over top half of bun with mayonnaise. Place on hamburger and serve. Yields 6 cheeseburgers.

Vegetables

Salads, Salad Dressings, and Garnishes

Preserves, Jellies, and Relishes

S ummer was the busy time back in the old days. There was corn to be gathered, hay to be cut, and the last chopping and weeding of the cotton before the crop was "laid by." (This meant there was nothing left to be done until the cotton bolls opened and it was ready to be picked.) There was an old saying that "if the cotton was lappin' in the middles on the Fourth of July, you will have a good crop."

We always celebrated the Fourth of July with a picnic, either down on the creek bank or in someone's back yard. We always barbecued a pig, and one time we barbecued a goat. My great-grandfather Fleming was always in charge of the Fourth of July picnic. They would always roast a suckling pig. Early in the day, he would dig a pit and get the fire going, and by afternoon he would set the pig up on the roasting pin.

Fourth of July Picnic
Roast Pig with Barbecue Sauce
Potato Salad
Greens and Corn bread
Roast Ears of Corn
Cakes and Pies
Watermelon

This is our most important holiday. The Fourth of July means freedom to blacks, freedom from slavery. Despite the fact that it really is America's Independence Day, the Fourth became associated in black people's minds with "Freedom Day." After the crop is "laid by," it is time for the Watch Meetings and the Protracted Meetings at the churches, which leads up to baptizing. These go on for a couple of weeks. In Grandma's time the men would come to the church from the fields, and the women would bring basket suppers — fried chicken, potato salad, biscuits, fried salt meat, and syrup, and always cakes and pies. All over Hollandale, you could hear the singing coming from the little churches. Now they have a week of prayer service and a week of preaching coming up to baptism. Bringing baskets of food unfortunately isn't done anymore.

This was also the time for preserving and canning. All the vegetables were coming in—tomatoes, okra, squash, cucumbers, peppers, watermelons, and green and red peppers. Soup mixtures were "put up," along with dill and sweet pickles, relishes and chow-chow. Plums, peaches, pears and figs were ripe.

It was also time for homemade ice cream. In the days before my time someone would go to town on Saturday and get a block of ice wrapped in a burlap sack which was stuffed with sawdust. This was put in the ice box, and they used an ice pick to chip off the ice when they were ready to make the homemade peach ice cream for Sunday dinner. The children helped turn the handle so they could get to lick the dasher. Now we use an electric ice cream freezer. Ice cream was generally made when the preachers came. They always loved to come to my great-grandmother Fleming's house, because she was well-known for her great meals, especially her fried chicken and her berry pies.

Vegetables

Gardens were a major source of food for the black family. I am convinced that if it had not been for raising many vegetables in the garden, black families' diets would not have been nutritious. The major source of vegetables were greens, peas (better known as crowders and purple hulls), speckled butter beans, and green (lima) beans. Rafters were placed in the garden for beans to run on, and stakes were placed around tomatoes, and as they grew, they would be tied with strings to the stakes.

Garden Fresh Butter Beans

5 to 8 slices salt pork
2 quarts butter beans
2½ quarts water
⅛ cup shortening or vegetable oil
1 tsp. salt
2 tsp. sugar

In a boiler, boil salt pork for 60 minutes at medium heat. Drain water from salt pork, and add the 2½ quarts of water, butter beans, shortening, salt, and sugar. Simmer at a low to medium heat for 90 minutes. Yields servings for 8 to 10 persons. Serve hot with corn bread.

Butter Bean Special with Okra

4 hock bones
1 pound frozen bag of butter beans
2½ quarts water
1 tsp. sugar
⅛ tsp. salt
¾ stick butter
½ tsp. pepper
10 pods okra

In a boiler, add hock bones and water, simmering for 2 hours. Add beans, sugar, salt, butter and pepper. Simmer for 60 minutes. Add okra on top of beans after seasonings have been added. After you have added the okra do not stir anymore. Allow to simmer uncovered. Yields 8 to 10 servings.

STORAGE OF BEANS AND PEAS

1 bushel of garden-fresh butter beans or purple hull peas
water
12 quart-size freezer bags

Shell beans or peas into a large dishpan and discard the hulls. Butter beans should be checked carefully for any debris that may have fallen into the pan by mistake. Place beans in a colander and, under cool running water, clean beans thoroughly. Drain water and fill each freezer bag ¾ full with beans or peas. Zip tight and freeze until ready to use.

Do not put a spoon in these beans after you have added the potatoes. Beans do not need to be stirred, and stirring will crumble the potatoes. I'm serious about this. It's important.

FREEZING SNAP BEANS

1 bushel of green beans
24 slices of salt pork, cooked for 30 minutes
2 T. salt water
8 gallon-size ziplock freezer bags

In a large dishpan snap the ends off green beans. Then place pan with beans into the sink, fill with cool water, and sprinkle salt in water. Allow to sit for 10 to 15 minutes. Then wash beans in two

Green Bean Sauté

5 slices bacon strips, grilled
fat from grilled bacon
2 cans #303 green beans
1 large onion, chopped
1 tsp. sugar
½ tsp. salt
⅛ tsp. butter or margarine

Empty beans and juices into a deep boiler, adding fat from bacon, with onions, sugar, salt, and butter. Simmer for 30 to 35 minutes, uncovered. Add bacon strips to top of beans and serve. Serves 5.

Green Beans and Potatoes

4 ham hocks
3½ quarts water
3 quarts string beans (fresh)
2 T. shortening (do not use oil)
2 tsp. sugar
1 tsp. salt
1 tsp. pepper
8 miniature white potatoes, peeled

In a deep boiler, simmer ham hocks and water for 1½ hours. Add beans, shortening, sugar, salt, pepper, and potatoes and cook partially uncovered on top of stove for 2 hours, or until tender, on medium heat. Serves 6 to 8. If you wish you can omit the potatoes from this recipe.

Kidney Beans

5 strips salt pork
3 quarts water
1-pound bag of red kidney beans
2 T. vegetable shortening
1 tsp. sugar
½ tsp. salt

Soak beans in warm water for 1 hour. Wash salt pork thoroughly of excess salt. Boil salt pork for 30 minutes in boiler with water. Add beans, shortening, sugar, and salt. Cook beans on medium heat for 2½ hours uncovered until tender. Serve over rice. Serves 5 to 6.

additional sinkfuls of water until clean. In freezer bags place 2 or 3 slices of salt pork along with beans, fillings bags. Freeze.

Black families have always provided for their families by growing their own good-tasting foods. Many items were derived from foods grown n trees or in the gardens or in the woods and fields. Among these items were figs, apples, plums, pears, peaches, pecans, walnuts, and persimmons grown on trees. In the garden, many vegetables were grown. Families raised big patches of musards, turnips, and collard greens, butter beans, lima beans, field peas or crowder peas, bell peppers, red peppers, cucumbers, okra, green and red tomatoes, corn, squash, beets, white or red potatoes, green beans, cabbage, sweet

Mama's Lima Beans

1-pound bag of dried lima beans
4 ham hocks
3½ quarts water
1 tsp. salt
1 tsp. sugar
2 T. shortening

Soak beans in warm water for 1 hour. Place ham hocks in boiler with water, simmering until tender for 3 hours. Add beans, salt, sugar, and shortening and cook for 90 minutes uncovered on medium heat. Serves 5 to 6.

Oven-Baked Pork and Beans

2 #303 cans pork and beans
½ cup syrup, ribbon cane
½ cup brown sugar
2 tsp. mustard
⅓ stick melted butter
6 slices bacon
2 cups barbecue sauce

Pour beans into pan, adding syrup, brown sugar, mustard, butter, bacon, and barbecue sauce, mixing well. Bake in oven for 1 hour at 350 degrees. Serves 6 to 8 persons.

Pinto Bean Supreme

1-pound bag of dried pinto beans
4 ham hocks
4 quarts water
2 tsp. sugar
2 T. shortening
1 tsp. salt
1½ tsp. chili powder

Soak beans in warm water for 1 hour. Boil ham hocks in water for 1 hour. Add beans, shortening, sugar, salt and chili powder. Simmer uncovered for 2½ hours. Serves 6 to 7 persons.

potatoes, green onions and green peas. Then there were those items that grow wild, such as wild greens, wild onions, blackberries, dewberries, wild grapes (sometimes called possum grapes), and muscadines. During the depression, some people made mulberry pies. (They said they were delicious but seedy.) From these fruits, nuts, and vegetables, many great nutritious meals were provided and many are still provided this way!

Adding bell pepper to cabbage makes it great. Try it and see.

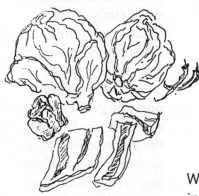

Cabbage and Salt Pork

2 hard heads of cabbage
8 slices salt pork
1½ quarts water
1 tsp. sugar
¼ tsp. salt
2 T. shortening
1 bell pepper, chopped (optional)
dash of red pepper, if desired

Wash cabbage, cutting into wedges. Fry salt pork in boiler, adding water. Simmer for 2 hours. Now add cabbage, sugar, salt and shortening, simmering for 20 to 25 minutes. Sprinkle crushed red pepper on top of cabbage, once tender. Serves 5 to 7.

Buttered Carrot Entré

8 whole carrots, scraped
1 quart water
1 tsp. salt
1 tsp. pepper
¾ stick butter

In a boiler, add water and carrots, salt, pepper, and butter. Boil for 1 hour or until tender on medium heat. Serves 4 persons.

Broccoli and Cheese Sauce

1 quart water
2 bunches fresh broccoli
¾ stick butter
2 tsp. salt
1 cup milk
2 cups Cheddar cheese

Cook broccoli in sauce pan or boiler until tender on medium heat adding butter and salt to the water. In a separate saucepan, stir in milk and cheese until cheese melts and milk disappears. Serve cheese sauce atop hot broccoli.

Boiled Corn, Southern Style

6 ears of corn
2 quarts boiling water
2 tsp. salt
4 T. butter
2 tsp. pimiento, if desired

Place corn in boiling water with 1 teaspoon salt. Boil for 30 minutes on medium heat. Remove corn to skillet with butter and sauté with butter. Serve with pimiento on top. Serves 6.

Fried Corn

Straight from the Garden

1 sharp knife
8 to 10 ears of shucked corn (fresh from the garden)
¾ cup flour
2 T. sugar
2 tsp. pepper
1 cup vegetable oil

With a sharp knife cut the end off of each ear of corn, so the ear will form a stand. Now take your knife and scrape the corn from the cob into a bowl. It will be milky and contain grains of corn. Add and mix in flour, sugar and pepper. Pour mixture into warmed vegetable oil and stir-fry until done. Cook about 20 to 30 minutes. Serve with your favorite meat. Yields servings for 3 or 4 persons.

When I was a kid and we would get dolls for Christmas, we would comb their hair so much, they were bald-headed by summertime. Their hair was always hard and tangly. So for mere entertaiment, we would take corn shucks and shred them real fine and make dolls' hair. Then we would stick the shredded shucks down in a coke bottle, and dress it up to make a doll. We would braid hair for days. We would comb and fix dolls' hair like we were in the beauty parlor business. Perhaps you may wonder about me and these dolls, but when I was a kid, I was afraid of real dolls. I guess I thought they'd finally speak to me one day.

Sunday's Fried Corn

2 #303 cans cream-style corn
½ cup vegetable oil
3 T. plain white flour
3 T. sugar
1 tsp. pepper

Pour corn into bowl and mix with flour, sugar, and pepper. Pour ingredients into skillet that has been preheated with oil. Stir-fry for 20 minutes. Serve with your favorite meat. Serves 5 to 6 persons.

Skillet-Fried Eggplant

2 quarts water
4 eggplants, cubed or sliced
1 onion, chopped
3 tsp. salt
3 tsp. pepper
1 cup vegetable oil

In a boiler, add eggplant, salt, pepper, and water. Simmer over medium heat for 35 to 40 minutes. Drain water from eggplant, add onions and pour into skillet which has been pre-warmed with the oil, and stir-fry for 20 minutes. Serve hot. Yields 7 to 8 servings.

Greens from the garden were always thought to be muscle food that would bring forth good health. Today, people still believe a nourishing meal must include garden-fresh greens.

Collard Greens Deluxe

3 bunches collard greens
4 ham hocks
3½ quarts water
4 T. vegetable shortening
1 T. sugar
1 tsp. salt

Pick, wash, and remove stems from greens. Boil ham hock for 1 hour in water. Do not drain. Add greens, shortening, sugar, and salt. Simmer for 2½ to 3 hours or until tender. The secret to perfect collards is to cook until very tender. Serves 6 to 7 persons.

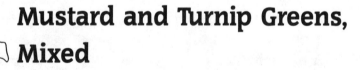

Mustard and Turnip Greens, Mixed

4 bunches mustards and turnips, mixed
8 strips salt pork
4 quarts water
3 T. shortening
2 tsp. sugar
1 tsp. salt

Pick greens, removing ¾ of the stems. Wash thoroughly 3 or 4 times in cool water. Wash salt pork thoroughly, and boil for 60 minutes. Add greens, shortening, sugar and salt. Simmer for 2 hours. Serves 6 persons.

Wild Greens Medley

8 slices salt pork

3 quarts water

2 quarts wild greens (2 bunches mustards and turnips can be substituted)

1 tsp. salt

2 tsp. sugar

2 T. vegetable shortening

cornmeal dumplings (recipe follows)

Wash and pick greens thoroughly, removing stems. In a deep boiler, boil salt meat for 45 minutes. Do not drain. Add greens to salt pork, with sugar and shortening, simmering for 2 hours. After the greens have simmered for 1 hour, add the balls of cornmeal dumplings by laying them on top of greens. Simmer for the last hour with top on the boiler. Yields servings for 6 to 8 persons.

Sometimes people would put spells on your cooking. Aunt Frances had a neighbor who was jealous of her, and she came by one day while Aunt Frances was cooking greens. The neighbor kept staring down in the greens pot, and when Aunt Frances started eating them she became real sick, and they had to call the two-headed man to make her well. The woman had put a spell on her, and it took the two-headed man to take it away. The two-headed man was like a witch doctor. Some people think this started in African culture, and when the village medicine man practiced his witchcraft he wore a mask. So some people think that's the way the two-headed man got his name.

In the days when times were truly hard, black families could always find some clabber milk in the ice box, some meal on the shelf, and wild greens. People did not have to plant wild greens. They grew religiously. The smell of wild greens in the grass was so strong-scented that it was always easy to find them. These were among the nutritious meals prepared. At the end of the month, when money was low, we still could have a delicious meal.

The salt is used to help remove any dirt granules or particles from the greens. The salt will make the dirt fall to the bottom of the sink. Use it in the first water only.

Dumplings

2 cups cornmeal
1 cup boiling hot water (must be boiling hot)
1 tsp. salt

Mix ingredients well, and make into small meatball-size dumplings.

Storage of Mustard and Turnip Greens

8 bunches or 1 dishpan of greens
4 T. salt
water
6 gallon-size ziplock freezer bags

Remove stems of greens and discard. Move greens to sink and fill it with cool running water. Sprinkle salt over greens and allow them to sit in salt water for 10 to 15 minutes. Wash greens thoroughly 2 or 3 times or until water is clear. Drain water off and place greens in freezer bags, filling them to the rim. Close tightly, freeze, and use as needed.

Lye Hominy

During the 1900s, my great-grandmother, Aunt Frances, began to sell lye hominy in jars to white families. In case you are wondering how she made the hominy, here is the recipe. I am sure you don't have a storage house of roasting ears as was the case then, but finding an ear of corn in the South, even today, is not impossible. First find the main items:

1 black cast-iron pot
8 to 9 ears roasting corn
1 pound stove ashes

Shell the corn from the ears, and put it in the pot with the ashes. Then put enough water in the pot to cover corn and ashes, stirring constantly until it comes to a boil. Boil until the hominy is fluffy and all of the corn is fully cooked from kernel to hominy. It will be a yellow, puffy ball. Place the hominy in a strainer and rinse until all of the ashes and husks are removed. The hominy should now be pretty and white.

The final procedure is now to get out a cast-iron skillet, put in a small amount of vegetable shortening, and brown the hominy. Remove and serve with butter atop your favorite meat, bacon, or salt pork.

This recipe is well over a 125 years old and it is proven to work.

Don't be confused about the ashes. You won't be eating them. As my grandmother explained, ashes have the same reaction as charcoal, which does filter things. The ashes purify and dehusk the corn.

In the old days, lye hominy was made outdoors in a big black pot and stirred with long wooden paddles.

Despite the fact that okra has little nutritional value, it is such a delicious treat, either fried or boiled, that okra was one of the main items planted in country gardens. Making soup without okra and stewed tomatoes is like baking a cake without baking powder. Tomatoes and okra were put up in jars for soup stock to last from one season to the next.

Boiled Okra

12 pods okra
3½ cups water
1 tsp. salt
1 tsp. pepper, more if desired

In a boiler, add okra, salt and pepper to water. Boil until tender, about 20 minutes. Drain. Serves 4 persons.

Southern Fried Okra

3 cups meal
15 to 20 pods okra
2 T. salt
2 T. pepper
2½ cups vegetable oil
3 eggs, beaten

Place meal in bowl, mixing in salt and pepper. Warm oil in skillet. Dip okra in eggs, then in meal mixture, and fry until golden brown. Serves 4 to 5 persons.

Black-Eyed Peas Delight

1 pound black-eyed peas (dried)
4 ham hocks
4 quarts water
2 T. vegetable shortening
2 tsp. sugar
1 tsp. salt

Soak peas in warm water for 1 hour, and drain. Boil ham hocks in water for 1 hour. Add peas, shortening, sugar, and salt. Simmer for 90 minutes. Serves 6 to 7 persons.

Crowder Field Peas

½ gallon field peas (crowders)
4 ham hocks
3 quarts water
2 T. vegetable shortening
1 tsp. salt
1 tsp. sugar
10 pods okra

In deep boiler, cook hock bones 1½ hours on medium heat. Remove hock bones from water, and boil peas for 30 minutes. Drain peas from water,

General advice:

If your vegetables haven't got a little thickening in them, you haven't cooked them right. The secret of this thickening is the oil or butter you put in them.

adding another three quarts of water to boiler. Put in hock bones, peas, vegetable shortening, salt and sugar. Simmer for 60 minutes. Add okra on top of peas. (Avoid stirring.) Simmer for 30 minutes longer. Serves 6 to 7 persons.

Garden Fresh English Peas with Carrots

6 to 8 slices salt pork
2 quarts water
2 quarts English peas (fresh)
1 tsp. salt
$\frac{1}{8}$ cup shortening or vegetable oil
2 tsp. sugar
2 cups carrots, cubed or sliced

In a deep boiler, add salt pork to water and boil for 90 minutes at medium heat. Drain water from salt pork and add the 2 quarts of water. Cook for 15 minutes at medium heat, adding peas, salt, sugar, and oil. Simmer over medium heat for 60 minutes. Add carrots and simmer for 30 minutes at medium heat. Yields servings for 7 to 8 persons.

Zesty English Peas

2 #303 cans English peas
1 T. sugar
½ tsp. pepper
1 T. butter

Drain juice from 1 can of peas. Put 2 cans of peas with juice from 1 can in heavy boiler. Add sugar, pepper, and butter. Simmer for 15 minutes. Serves 5 to 6 persons.

Baked Potatoes with Chives and Cheese

5 Irish potatoes (white)
5 T. sour cream
½ cup vegetable shortening
¾ cup chives
5 tsp. butter
5 tsp. bacon bits
5 slices American cheese
5 pieces foil

Grease each potato with shortening and wrap tightly in foil. Place in a roasting pan and bake for 90 minutes at 375 degrees. Remove potatoes from

Sweet potatoes were dug and piled up under a shed and covered over with hay. This was called a "sweet potato pump" and you would leave an opening so you could reach in and get your sweet potatoes, and then cover the opening back up with hay, so the potatoes would not freeze.

oven, split open, and stuff with sour cream, chives, butter, and bacon bits. Top with cheese. Grill in bottom section of oven for 2 to 3 minutes. Serves 5 persons.

Baked Sweet Potatoes

6 medium sweet potatoes
½ cup vegetable shortening
6 tsp. butter

Wash sweet potatoes, and grease the outside of the potatoes thoroughly. Place on cookie sheet, and bake in oven at 325 degrees for 2½ to 3 hours. Split open each potato and add one tablespoon of butter before eating. Makes a great dessert. Will serve 5 to 6 persons.

Hash Brown Potatoes

4 white potatoes (Irish)
2 cups vegetable oil
1½ T. salt

Grate potatoes and add salt. Place potatoes in skillet
of warm oil, and fry until golden brown. Serve hot.
Serves 4 to 5 persons.

Southern Creamed Potatoes

6 medium white potatoes, sliced
2½ quarts water
2 tsp. salt
½ cup evaporated milk
2 T. butter

Peel and slice potatoes. Boil in water for 45 minutes.
Drain water from potatoes. and mash until all lumps
have disappeared. Add salt, milk, and butter, cream-
ing until smooth. Serves 5 to 6 persons.

Out of necessity, black families thought up all kinds of ways to cook potatoes. This is one of the easiest, cheapest, but still most delicious ways of cooking potatoes.

Stewed Potatoes

6 medium white potatoes
2 medium onions, sliced
¾ cup oil
2 tsp. salt
2 tsp. pepper
1½ cups water

Peel potatoes and onions. Slice ½-inch thick. Stir-fry in oil until slightly browned. Add salt, pepper, and water, and simmer uncovered for 60 minutes. Serves 5 to 6 persons.

Steamed Rice

2 cups rice
water
2 T. vinegar

In a boiler, pour in rice, touch rice with the tip of your index finger, and add water until it reaches the first line of that finger. Never let the water pass that line. Stir in the vinegar. Cover with a top and steam on medium heat until ¾ of the water has cooked out. Then remove the top and continue to steam on low heat until rice is dry and fluffy. The finger measure will ensure your rice will not be soggy. The vinegar will make it pretty and white.

Hint: If you run out of vinegar and you're in a rush, you can substitute buttermilk or lemon juice.

Stewed Squash

6 medium squash, yellow
2 small onions
¾ cup vegetable oil
1 T. salt
1 tsp. pepper
1½ cups water

Wash and slice squash about ½ inch thick, and thinly slice onions. Pour oil into skillet. When warm, add squash, onions, salt, and pepper. Brown and stir-fry for 10 minutes. Add water, and simmer for 30 to 40 minutes uncovered, stirring occasionally. Serves 5 to 6 persons.

Green tomatoes are better once the frost hits them.

Home-Fried Green Tomatoes

4 green tomatoes (sliced to thickness desired)
2½ cups white cornmeal
3 tsp. salt
1½ tsp. pepper
2 cups vegetable oil

Mix meal, salt, and pepper. Dip sliced tomatoes in meal mixture, and cover them evenly on both sides. Warm oil, and fry each side to a golden brown. Serves 5 persons.

Tomatoes and Okra, Stewed

1 quart red tomatoes, sectioned
1 quart okra, cut
2 cups onions, chopped
2 T. vegetable oil
1 T. salt
1½ tsp. pepper
2 cups water

In a skillet, warm oil, adding tomatoes, okra and onions. Sprinkle salt and pepper evenly over mixture. Stir-fry for 15 minutes in skillet. Add water and simmer for 25 to 30 minutes. Serve hot. Yields 6 to 8 servings.

Stuffed Tomatoes

5 medium tomatoes
3 cups ground beef
1 cup onions, chopped
1 cup bell peppers, chopped
2 tsp. salt
⅛ cup pimiento
5 slices of American cheese

If you want to add the inner portion of the tomato to the ground beef, you can do so.

Cut top off tomatoes and hull out inner portion to form a cup. In a skillet, stir-fry ground beef, adding onions, bell peppers, salt, and pepper, stirring until browned. Mix in pimientos and stuff tomatoes with mixture, placing a slice of cheese on each tomato. Put in oven, and bake at 350 degrees for 20 to 25 minutes. Sprinkle top with paprika for decoration. Serves 5.

Homemade Fresh Vegetable Mix for Soup

½ gallon garden-fresh butter beans, shelled
2 gallons okra, cut
8 ears of corn, kernels grated from ear
12 medium-ripe tomatoes, peeled

This was used to make soup for Blue Monday goers at Fair Deals Cafe.

4 quarts water

6 T. salt

12 quart-size freezer bags (or quart jars)

Shell and wash butter beans. Add cut okra, grated corn, cut tomatoes, and water. Cook in deep boiler on top of stove over low heat for 45 minutes. Add salt during the cooking period. Place stock in quart-size bags or jars, for freezing. Yields 12 to 14 quarts.

Pickled Beets, Delta Style

12 small beets, peeled

1½ quarts water

2 cups sugar

1 cup vinegar

1 tsp. butter

1 tsp. salt

Wash beets thoroughly. Peel and slice, adding to a boiler with water, sugar, vinegar, butter, and salt. Cook on medium heat for 30 minutes or until tender. Leave out to cool. Refrigerate to chill. Serves 6 to 7.

Salads, Salad Dressings, and Garnishes

Carrot-Raisin Salad

4 carrots, grated
¾ cup mayonnaise
1½ cups apple chunks
1 T. sugar
dash of salt
1 cup raisins

Grate carrots finely, adding mayonnaise, apple chunks, sugar, salt, and raisins, stirring all ingredients until mixed well. Chill and serve. Yields 5 to 6 servings.

Celery Seed Dressing

⅓ cup lemon juice
½ cup vinegar
⅓ cup Karo light syrup
½ cup celery seeds
⅓ cup sugar
¼ cup vegetable oil
1 cup confectioners sugar

Mix lemon juice, vinegar, syrup, celery seed, sugar, oil and confectioners sugar. Mix well and serve over fruits and vegetables.

Stuffed Celery Sticks

1 stalk of celery
2 cups peanut butter
½ cup confectioners sugar
1 cup pimiento cheese spread
paprika

Stuffing Mix

In a bowl, mix peanut butter and confectioners sugar together until creamy. Wash celery thoroughly, cutting each stem into half-strips, and removing ends. In the center of each stick, stuff with peanut butter, and at each end, stuff with pimiento cheese. Sprinkle with paprika for decoration.

Combination Salad

1 head of lettuce
3 tomatoes, sectioned
¼ cup bell pepper rings
½ cup onion rings
6 radishes, sliced
1 cup carrots, grated
½ tsp. sugar
½ cup cheese, grated
1 cup mayonnaise, or preferably salad dressing
1½ tsp. salt

Wash lettuce thoroughly and shred. Add tomatoes, bell pepper rings, onion, radishes, carrots, sugar, and cheese. Mix with mayonnaise and salt. Serve in individual bowls. Yields 6 to 8 six-ounce bowls.

Ham and Cheese Salad

1 head of lettuce
8 slices cooked ham, chopped
6 slices crisp bacon
3 tomatoes, sectioned
6 slices American or hoop cheese, cubed
1½ tsp. salt
1 cup mayonnaise

Wash and shred lettuce and place in salad bowl. Brown ham slightly, and broil bacon to crispness. Cut ham in 1½-inch cubes, and cut bacon into four-piece sections. Add tomatoes, cheese, salt and mayonnaise to salad bowl. Toss salad, adding ham and cheese and bacon last. Chill and serve. Yields servings for 5 to 6 persons.

Macaroni Salad

3 quarts water
4 cups elbow macaroni
1 cup salad dressing
½ cup sweet pickle relish
½ cup pimientos, chopped
1 T. sugar
1 tsp. salt

½ cup bell pepper, finely chopped
¼ cup onions
1 tsp. mustard

Boil macaroni for 20 minutes. Drain and place in a bowl, adding salad dressing, relish, pimientos, sugar, salt, bell pepper, onions, and mustard. Refrigerate and chill. Yields 6 to 7 servings.

This potato salad recipe was developed by my great-grandmother. It's the greatest.

AUNT FRANCES' SALAD OIL

After hog killings, Aunt Frances would take some of the pork skins, and put them in deep cookie sheets in the oven, and bake them until the skins were crisp and the oil drained out. Then she would strain the oil through calico or gingham until clear. The skins were eaten as pork rinds for a snack, and the oil saved for salad dress-ings and for special cooking.

Potato Salad

5 medium white potatoes
2 quarts water
3 eggs
½ cup salad dressing
2 T. sugar
¼ cup onions, chopped
2 T. mustard
3 to 4 ounces sweet pickle relish

Peel potatoes and slice. Put sliced potatoes and whole eggs in a boiler of cool water. Boil for 15 to 20 minutes, or until potatoes are ready for mashing. Drain water from potatoes thoroughly. Mash and add salad dressing, sugar, onions, mustard, and pickle relish. Mix well. Add the hard-boiled eggs which have had the shells removed and have been chopped. Refrigerate and serve. Yields 10 to 12 servings.

Shrimp Salad

4 beds of lettuce in salad plates
24 medium shrimp, boiled in seasoning salt
¾ cup cream cheese
¼ cup sour cream
½ tsp. sugar
⅛ tsp. salt
1 cup celery, chopped
¼ cup bell pepper, finely chopped
⅛ cup pimientos

In a bowl, add shrimp, cream cheese, sour cream, sugar, salt, celery, bell pepper, and pimientos. Mix well, serving on beds of lettuce. Yields servings for 4 persons.

Slaw

1 large head green cabbage, shredded
½ cup purple head cabbage, shredded
½ cup onions, finely chopped
1 cup sweet pickle relish
¼ cup sugar
1 cup salad dressing
1 small carrot, grated
⅛ tsp. salt

Wash cabbage before shredding. In a large bowl, add to cabbage, onions, relish, sugar, salad dressing, carrots, and salt. Mix thoroughly, and chill. Yields 8 to 10 servings.

Tuna Salad on Lettuce

2 8-ounce cans chunky light tuna
2 T. sugar
$\frac{1}{8}$ tsp. salt
$\frac{1}{4}$ cup mayonnaise
2 eggs, boiled and chopped
$\frac{1}{4}$ cup sweet pickle relish
$\frac{1}{8}$ cup onions, finely chopped
paprika

Drain oil from tuna. Add sugar, salt, mayonnaise, chopped eggs, relish, and onions, mixing well. Chill and serve on lettuce leaves, sprinkling paprika on top to decorate. Serves 4 to 5.

Homemade Thousand Island Dressing

2 cups mayonnaise or salad dressing
1 cup tomato catsup
½ cup sweet pickle relish
1½ T. sugar
⅛ tsp. salt
3 tsp. herb seasoning

Place mayonnaise in small bowl, stirring in catsup, pickle relish, sugar, salt and spices. Mix well, chill, and serve. Will spread 4 to 6 salads.

Black families had many substitutes for unaffordable items, and this method is designed to be a substitute for 1000 Island dressing.

Preserves, Jellies, and Relishes

All jars, lids and rings should be washed carefully and rinsed in scalding water.

Sweet Buttered Pickles

24 medium-sized cucumbers (about 5″ long)
1 gallon vinegar
1 stick butter
2 T. allspice
4 pounds sugar
6 to 8 quart jars

In deep dishpan, add vinegar, washed cucumbers, butter, sugar and allspice. Cook for 90 minutes or until tender. Use quart-size canning jars, adding juice and 3 to 4 pickles to a jar. Put aside with lids almost tight until cool. After cooling, tighten jars and put away on shelves. In most cases the longer the shelf lifetime, the better the pickles.

Chow-Chow

24 medium green tomatoes, chopped
4 medium onions, chopped
5 pounds cabbage, chopped
2 quarts vinegar
⅓ cup salt
⅛ cup pepper
1½ cups sugar
2½ T. crushed red pepper (if desired)
½ cup allspice
12 pint jars

Chop all above ingredients indicated. In a large bowl, mix vinegar, salt, pepper, sugar, crushed red pepper, and allspice to all chopped ingredients. Simmer for 2½ to 3 hours over medium heat, stirring constantly until tender. Set aside to cool, and add to jars. Yields 10 to 12 pint jars.

The southern pronunciation of this is cha-cha.

The green tomato vines were always found to make a second bunch of tomatoes. It was always considered that once the frost fell on the first bunch of green tomatoes, they were tender and ready for frying and chow-chow.

Plum Jelly

2 pecks of plums
10 pounds sugar
water enough to cover plums in pan
1 to 2 boxes gelatin, unflavored

Wash plums thoroughly. Place plums in a large dishpan, and cover with water. Simmer for 2 hours. Once you have finished cooking these plums, a whitish film will appear on top. Strain the plums and juices through cheesecloth, squeezing until all liquids are removed. Once all juices have been strained, prepare to mix jelly: for every 1 cup of plum juice, add 1 cup of sugar. After mixing and measuring all juices, now add Sure-Jell, stirring well and simmering on stovetop until juices turn to a jellylike solution. Makes 24 pints.

Testing Results: Take out some juice of the plum jelly, about ⅓ cup, and place in a bowl. Once the juice turns to jelly, it is ready to be put in jars, with lids loosened until completely cooled. Then tighten jar tops.

Suggestions: In grocery markets, you can buy a wax used for sealing jellies and preserves.

Fig Preserves

2 pecks of fresh figs (almost ripe)
8 pounds sugar
2 small lemons, sliced thin
½ cup cloves
12 pint jars

Remove stems and wash figs thoroughly. Place figs in a dishpan, and pour sugar over evenly. Let figs stand at room temperature overnight. The next morning, stir all ingredients, adding lemons and cloves, simmering on low heat for 60 to 90 minutes, or until juices are syrupy and thick. Yields approximately 10 to 12 pints of fig preserves.

Canning Procedure: Cool in jars with lids loosely fitted until completely cooled. Afterwards close tightly and place on shelf, using as desired.

Peach Preserves

1 bushel fresh peaches (almost ripe)
10 pounds sugar
¼ cup cloves
12 quart jars

Peel and slice peaches in quarter sections, removing all pits. Add sugar and soak on table-top overnight. The next morning, stir in the sugar carefully, and simmer over low heat for 2½ hours, stirring constantly to avoid sticking. Add cloves and cook for an additional 30 minutes, stirring constantly. Add preserves to jars, tightening tops loosely. Once peaches have cooled, tighten jars and place on shelf. Yields 10 to 12 quarts of preserves.

During the days when people had only a little, throwing things away was considered bad luck, so everything that could possibly be kept and used for a source of food was preserved.

Don't throw those hulls away! When you make peach preserves, save the hulls for peach brandy.

Pear Preserves

1 bushel fresh ripe pears
10 pounds sugar
¼ cup cloves
⅓ cup lemon rinds
12 quart jars

Peel and slice pears, covering with sugar, and let stand overnight, on table-top or in pantry. The next morning, stir pears and sugar together and add lemon rinds, cooking over low heat until syrup is real thick, for approximately 3 hours. Stir constantly to avoid sticking. At least 20 to 30 minutes before completion of cooking, add cloves, stirring well, then add preserves to jars. Close every top very loosely until cool, then tighten. Yields 12 jars.

Brandy (Peach)

1 gallon water
1 gallon peach hulls
5 pounds sugar

In dishpan, boil hulls, sugar and water for 90 minutes, stirring constantly. Remove from heat and set aside on tabletop in a cool place for 2 or 3 days. Check the mixture daily. This is important. Temperature and altitude will determine brandying time and the actual aging process. How do you know when it's ready? Once the brandy develops a smell of alcohol, you can chill, or store in jars, and serve as desired. Yields 5 or 6 quarts.

Cranberry Sauce

1-pound bag raw whole cranberries
2 cups sugar
1½ quarts water

Cook cranberries in water and sugar for 1½ hours, or until hulls have departed from the whole cranberries. Allow to drain in a strainer. Pour into bowl and allow to cool. Refrigerate and serve.

FALL

Breads and Rolls
Desserts

This is the most important time of the year — the time the farmers are getting the crop out (harvesting the cotton). It used to be that everybody was picking cotton—men, women, and children going up and down the cotton rows, dragging the long sacks from sunup to sun-down. Wagons went back and forth to the gin and the oil mill. The pickers brought their lunches, a bucket of water, and quilts to put down for the babies under a nearby tree. Sometimes there was a leader (called an Eagle Rocker) who'd lean on the back of his hoe and start a song, and the others would answer. This made the long day go faster. Picking went on from late summer into fall.

This was the money crop, and it was important to get all the cotton out before the heavy rains and the bad weather set in.

Pecans were beginning to fall. Persimmons were turning yellow. The older folks remember purple possum grapes and bronzy muscadines hanging from the tops of the tall trees. It was time to dig the sweet potatoes and put them in the sweet potato pump. The little shed next to the corn crib would be full of baskets of Irish potatoes, sprinkled over with lime to preserve them, black-eyed peas, crowder (field) peas, green tomatoes, onions, strings of red peppers, pumpkins, and cushaws.

Thanksgiving came in the middle of cotton-picking time, but everyone would enjoy a nice turkey or goose, and sometimes, like in the depression, they would be glad to have a juicy fat hen. After Thanksgiving, everyone was working on winding up the crop and waiting for settlement day. Around Christmas I can remember the farmers who were regulars at the Fair Deal Cafe would be excited about their bonuses—lump sums of money from the crop. We were excited too, since this meant more money for the cafe. Women and children were busy cooking and baking, cracking and picking out pecans and walnuts, getting ready for Christmas. This was the most joyous holiday of the year. It was time for family members to come home on visits and old friends and neighbors to take Christmas together.

Here is my grandmama's and my Christmas dinner menu. The holiday table is never considered complete if you can't fill up at least one separate table with food. She used to start cooking five or six days before Christmas, starting with her cakes, and she would cook steady coming up to Christmas.

Christmas Dinner Main Course
Baked Turkey
Baked Duck
Baked Ham
Duck Dressing with Giblet Gravy
Potato Salad
Cranberry Sauce
Chow-Chow
Mustard and Turnip Greens
with Salt Meat and Ham Hocks
Corn Bread
Yeast Rolls
Dessert
Coconut Cake
Jelly Cake
Caramel Cake
Pecan Pies
Sweet Potato Pies
Ambrosia
Fruit Cake

Beverages
Egg Nog
Iced Tea
Beer/Wine
Soda

Breads and Rolls

Homemade Fist Biscuits

How to Fist a Biscuit:
Roll dough into a long roll, until it resembles a rolling pin. Flour lightly, placing dough in hand, pinching off one inch of end of dough. Roll in palms of your hands. Flatten to a round biscuit, placing onto greased pan. Repeat until all biscuits are made. Sometimes dough will get sticky to touch. Dust hand into flour and proceed.

5 cups flour (see note), sifted well
2 tsp. baking powder
½ tsp. salt
⅛ tsp. sugar
⅛ tsp. soda
1 heaping cup shortening
2 cups buttermilk

(Note: Save 1½ cups of flour for kneading and rolling.) Sift 3½ cups flour until light and fluffy into large bowl, adding baking powder, salt, sugar and soda. Mix ingredients well. Add shortening and buttermilk, alternating, until mixed well.

Use the remaining flour to roll out biscuits. Put the extra cup and a half of flour out on your board or wherever you will roll out the dough. (I use my kitchen table.) You will keep your hands dusted with flour and work more flour into the dough as you knead it. Knead and roll until kneading process is complete. You should knead the dough for about 5 or 6 minutes—until the dough no longer sticks to your fingers. Roll biscuits out to cut, or fist the biscuit. Place in a greased pan, and bake at 375 degrees for 15 minutes. Makes 24 biscuits.

Hoecake

When you have made all the biscuits you need, take the last part of the dough to make a hoecake or two. A hoecake is just a big wad of leftover dough. It may be as big as a salad plate. You just put it on the pan and cook it along with the other biscuits. A hoecake can also be made of corn bread.

My great-grandma thought that if you rolled a biscuit once it had been kneaded, it was a disgrace to the dough. And somehow she believed if you used your hands to fist a biscuit, it was a sign of honor and respect. I believe she thought it wasn't really good if you didn't get your hands in it.

You can cook a corn bread hoecake on top of the stove in the skillet, just like you make a flap jack or a pancake. When they are thick, we call them hoecakes.

You can make a wonderful corn cake with this same batter by pouring very thin into the skillet.

A black cast-iron skillet is a must!

One of the most exciting changes in cooking was converting from the wood-burning stove to the conventional gas and electric stove. Yet, now the microwave oven has been invented for the super-mom of today. Cooking with super heat instead of the traditional way causes simmering time to be lost, which, in my opinion destroys much of the great taste.

Many great dishes prepared by my great-grandmother were made on the old cast-iron wood-burning range we called a Jeff Davis stove. Wood was cut the exact size to fit the wood box. There were two to

Homemade Corn Bread

2½ cups plain white cornmeal
1 cup plain white flour
1½ tsp. sugar
⅓ tsp. salt
⅓ cup vegetable oil or bacon fat
2 eggs
2½ cups buttermilk

In a large bowl place meal, flour, sugar, salt, oil, eggs and buttermilk, beating well. Place in a skillet of warmed oil, and bake for 30 to 40 minutes or until firm, at 375 degrees. Serves 6.

Cracklin Corn Bread

2 cups cracklins (see page 12 for cracklin recipe)
2½ cups plain white cornmeal
1½ cups plain white flour
1 tsp. sugar
⅛ tsp. salt
2 eggs beaten
¼ cup melted vegetable oil
2½ cups buttermilk

Soak cracklins in warm water for 15 minutes. In a large bowl, place meal, flour, sugar, salt, eggs, oil and buttermilk, beating well. Drain excess water from the cracklins. Add cracklins to the batter last, and bake for 35 minutes at 375 degrees. Yields 6 slices.

Pepper Corn Bread

1 cup plain flour, sifted
1 cup plain corn meal, sifted
1 cup evaporated milk
2 tsp. baking powder
1 tsp. sugar
dash of salt
¼ cup vegetable oil
2 eggs, beaten
2 T. jalapeno peppers or hot peppers off the
   vine, chopped

Combine all ingredients except baking powder, milk, and pepper. Pour milk into mixture. Add baking powder on top and beat steadily for 5 minutes. Then add peppers. Pour into well-greased bread or muffin pan. Bake at 375 degrees for 20 minutes. Yields 8 to 10 servings.

four eyes on the top where heat could be controlled by moving the eyes half open or closed, or moving pots and pans back and forth from one heat to another. Warmers were on the top part of the stove, and there was a damper that you could move back and forth to control the heat. Sometimes it was on the oven door, and you had three heats: high, medium, and low. Sometimes there was a glass temperature gauge on the outer part of the stove. Learning how to measure heat on the old wood stoves was an art you had to acquire. After the electric and gas stoves became popular, people would laugh about cooking on those old Jeff Davis stoves.

Cornmeal Dumpling Medley

2 cups plain meal, sifted
1½ tsp. salt
1 cup boiling hot water

Mix meal and salt in a large bowl. Stir in hot water until you form a stiffness for rolling into a ball similar to a Swedish meatball. Drop dumplings into greens that are about half done and cook fully for about 1 hour. Makes about 12 or 15 dumplings.

Homemade Dumplings

3 cups plain flour, sifted
2 eggs
1 tsp. salt
½ cup water

Place flour in bowl, stirring in eggs, salt and water, stirring constantly, until mixed well. Let stand for 60 minutes or less. Place mixture on floured board and roll out as thin as possible. Cut in 2½-inch stringlike strips or squares, or as desired. Drop each dumpling into a hot broth, and cook on medium heat for 40 to 45 minutes.

Taking small food items and making delicious meals was a cultural art in the black family.

Hushpuppies

2½ cups cornmeal mix
1 T. vegetable oil and 3 cups for deep frying
1 cup onions, chopped
½ cup bell peppers, chopped
1⅓ cups buttermilk

In a bowl, mix cornmeal, oil, chopped onions, and bell pepper. Mix well with buttermilk until firm for rounding off to hushpuppies. Heat 3 cups of vegetable oil in deep fryer, dropping hushpuppies in singly and frying them until they are a golden brown. Yields 10 or 12.

Cornmeal mix is packaged meal with baking powder already added.

Miz Laura's Yeast Rolls

½ cup sugar
½ cup vegetable shortening
1¼ cups milk
1 package active yeast
2 cups cake flour, plain
1 tsp. baking powder
1 tsp. salt
½ tsp. soda

You can bake these rolls immediately, but they will be light as a feather if you wait till tommorrow.

Place sugar and shortening in milk, allowing it to get just warm enough to melt shortening. Set aside and allow to cool. (If the milk solution is too warm, it will kill the strength of the active yeast.) Add yeast to milk and stir until dissolved. Now you should sift flour into mixture until it is slightly juicy. Set aside, and allow dough to rise to top of bowl. Once it has risen, add baking powder, salt, and soda. Using your hands, work mixture into dough. Place dough on aluminum foil, sprinkle flour onto foil, and work in only enough flour to allow you to handle the dough with your hands. (Do not add too much flour. It will cause biscuits to be tough, so be careful.) Place into a buttered plastic bag. Refrigerate and cook tomorrow at 375 degrees. This will make 24 rolls or a nice loaf of bread.

Ten-Minute Homemade Cinnamon Slice

4 slices white bread
1 cup butter, melted
1 cup brown sugar
4 tsp. cinnamon
1 cup raisins

Spread bread on cookie sheet and butter face side up. Sprinkle with brown sugar evenly. Then sprinkle on cinnamon and raisins. Cover with sugar sauce (below). Put in oven for 4 to 5 minutes. Serve with coffee or milk.

Desserts

Among black families, one of the delicacies of food was red dirt from the hills. It was like a snack food. Whenever someone would come home from the hills, they would bring boxes of the clay for issuing out to friends for eating. I stopped eating dirt when I was fifteen years old, when I learned there might be certain impurities in the soil. Still, on a rainy day when I smell the rain aginst the dirt, I feel the hunger for some country red dirt.

Sugar Sauce

2 cups confectioners sugar
¼ cup lemon juice

Mix confectioners sugar and lemon juice to form a topping.

Ten-Minute Oven Pecan Brittle

2½ cups pecans, shelled
1 tsp. salt
¼ stick butter
1½ cups ribbon cane syrup

Take a cookie sheet and place pecans evenly onto pan. Sprinkle with salt and melted butter. Cover with syrup and place in oven for 10 to 15 minutes at 375 degrees or until bubbly. Cool and serve.

Mrs. Hunter's Southern Tea Cakes

2 cups sugar
3 eggs
1½ cups sweet milk
1½ tsp. baking powder
¾ stick butter
1½ tsp. nutmeg
3 cups plain white flour, sifted
2 tsp. vanilla flavoring

Beat sugar and eggs together for 15 minutes, adding milk, baking powder, butter, nutmeg, and vanilla. Roll onto a floured board and knead for about 5 minutes. Cut into ½-inch biscuit rounds, rolling out thin. Bake at 350 to 375 degrees for 15 to 20 minutes, or until cakes are firm. Yields 30 to 40 tea cakes.

Old-Fashioned Egg Custard

4 egg yolks and whites
1½ cups sugar
1 stick butter or margarine
1 cup evaporated milk
1 T. vanilla extract
1 tsp. cinnamon

In the old days, and back in the thirties, black families were too poor to have fancy chocolate chip cookies, but Lord, how good is an old-fashioned tea cake from a dishpan covered with cheesecloth.

The water for thickening should always be cool and the flour stirred in carefully. If your water is warm, the thickening is likely to lump.

Thickening:
  ½ cup cool water
  ⅛ cup flour, plain

Separate eggs, and beat egg yolks. Blend sugar, butter and milk, alternating one over the other. Add cinnamon and vanilla extract. Stir in egg yolks. Whip egg whites and add to mixture, then add thickening and pour into a greased pie pan or custard dish. Bake at 350 degrees for 40 minutes, and serve after cooling. Yields 5 to 6 custard dishes.

Homemade Vanilla Ice Cream

6 eggs, beaten
2 pounds sugar
2 gallons milk
2 T. vanilla flavoring
water and flour for thickening

In a bowl, add beaten eggs and sugar, cream well until smooth. (Just as if you were making a cake.) Now add your milk, flavoring, and thickening. Stir well. Place entire mixture on top of stove, and cook until it is very thick. Then pour into ice cream freezer bowl. Place bowl into electric freezer containing ice, turn on freezer and run until ice cream is hardened. This yields 2 gallons. Can be topped with peaches or strawberries, and cream, as desired.

Banana Pudding

4 egg yolks and whites, separated
1 can evaporated milk
2¼ cups sugar
1¼ cups water
¾ cup plain white flour
2 tsp. vanilla
5 cups vanilla wafers
6 medium-sized bananas (ripe)

In a boiler, beat egg yolks until they foam on top. Stir in milk, sugar and water. Stir constantly on low heat. The pudding mixture will thicken if you add flour slowly as you stir. Add vanilla. In a deep baking dish, add a layer of vanilla wafers, a layer of bananas, and a layer of pudding. Add two more layers of wafers, bananas and pudding. Top with meringue (see recipe on page 167). Brown and serve. Serves 7 to 8 persons.

In the old days there was always a nutmeg grater hanging beside the cook stove to liven up puddings and custards.

Rice Pudding

3 cups rice, cooked
1 cup evaporated milk
2 cups sugar
3 eggs
1 T. vanilla
1 tsp. baking powder
1¼ sticks butter

Place rice in bowl, adding cream, sugar, eggs, vanilla, baking powder, and melted butter, mixing ingredients well. Place in a round baking pan. Bake at 350 degrees for 45 minutes until firm. Serves 7 to 8 persons. Good with lemon icing over top.

Bread Pudding with Whiskey Sauce

12 slices stale bread
1½ cups water
2 cups sugar
3 eggs
1 cup evaporated milk
1 T. vanilla
1 stick butter or margarine
1 tsp. baking powder

Place bread in pan. Cover with water and soak for 5 minutes. Squeeze water from bread and place in bowl, adding sugar, eggs, cream, vanilla, melted butter or margarine, and baking powder. Stir well and bake for 40 to 45 minutes, or until firm, at 350 degrees. Serves 10 to 12. Serve with Lemon Whiskey Sauce (see below).

Lemon Whiskey Sauce

1 cup confectioners sugar
½ cup lemon juice
⅓ tsp. lemon extract
2 T. sugar
½ cup raisins
½ cup best whiskey

Thickening:
½ cup cold water
2 T. flour

In a boiler, put confectioners sugar, lemon juice, lemon extract, sugar, raisins, whiskey and thickening. Bring to a hard boil for 5 minutes. Serve over favorite pudding or rolls.

The tradition of not throwing away good food is followed in these recipes which use old white bread, corn bread, and leftover rice.

In my recipes you will not find cornstarch. But I want your gravies and thickening to be superb. Wait! Never mix hot water with flour for thickening; it must always be cool to keep the lumps out.

153

Where can we get "sweet milk"? Southerners use "sweet milk" to mean the opposite of buttermilk. Sweet milk is regular whole milk.

Pound Cake

1 cup and 1 tsp. butter, softened
2⅔ cups sugar
½ cup oil
4 eggs, beaten
3⅓ cups sifted flour, preferably plain cake flour
1 tsp. salt
1 cup sweet milk (white)
1½ tsp. baking powder
dash of baking soda

Cream butter, sugar, and oil until creamy, and there are no signs of a sugary feeling. Add eggs, beating for 1 to 2 minutes. Sift in 2⅔ cups flour and the salt, alternating with milk. Fold in baking powder and soda with the remaining ⅔ cup flour. Pour into a greased and floured cake pan, baking for 55 minutes at 325 degrees. Yields approximately 20 slices.

Pineapple Upside Down Cake

I use a basic pound cake for most of my cakes.

Pound cake recipe from page 154
2 cups brown sugar
2 cups crushed pineapple
3 bananas

In an oblong (9-inch) cake pan, cover bottom of pan evenly with brown sugar. Then pour pineapple evenly over brown sugar. Slice bananas over pineapple. Pour cake mix over bananas and bake for 50 to 55 minutes at 375 degrees. Cool and serve. Yields 24 slices.

Caramel Cake

Ice a pound cake with caramel frosting on page 157.

Lemon Rind Pound Cake

1 cup and 1 tsp. butter, softened
2⅔ cups sugar
½ cup oil
4 eggs, beaten

3 T. lemon rinds, grated, with juice
3⅓ cups flour, sifted (preferably plain cake flour)
1 tsp. salt
1 cup sweet milk (white)
1½ tsp. baking powder
Dash of baking soda

Cream butter, sugar, and oil until creamy, and there are no signs of a sugary feeling. Add eggs, beating for 1 to 2 minutes. Stir in lemon rinds and juice. Sift in 2⅔ cups flour and the salt, alternating with milk. Fold in baking powder and soda with the remaining ⅔ cup flour. Pour into a greased and floured cake pan, baking for 55 minutes at 325 degrees. Yields about 20 slices.

Coconut Cake

Use Pound Cake recipe on page 154
1 10-ounce can coconut or fresh coconut
vanilla frosting

Bake cake in layers. Cover with vanilla frosting (see recipe on page 159) and top with coconut. Cover each layer singly, adding final layer with frosting, and cover entire cake with coconut. Yields 18 to 20 slices.

Caramel Frosting

2 cups brown sugar
2 T. sweet milk
1 T. (heaping) vegetable shortening
2 cups confectioners sugar
1½ T. evaporated milk

In a double boiler, add brown sugar, milk, and shortening. Put on stove and stir ingredients for 5 minutes until mixed well. Cook at high heat until bubbly. Place the mixture aside until cooled to a warm state. Sift confectioners sugar into mixture, beating at medium speed until you obtain desired fluffiness. Allow to cool completely. Most of the time this frosting will have gotten hard. Add evaporated milk until it reaches the desired fluffiness. Frost cake as bundt or layer cake. Serves 20 persons.

Nutty Cream Cheese Frosting

6 ounces sour cream
1 T. lemon juice
2 egg whites
1½ cups confectioners sugar
1 T. milk
1 8-ounce cup cream cheese
1½ cups pecan pieces

In a bowl, add sour cream, lemon juice, egg whites, and sugar, beating until all ingredients are mixed well. Slightly warm milk and cream cheese in a saucepan. Combine both mixtures. If not fluffy, add confectioners sugar for desired consistency. Add nuts and spread over favorite cake. Will spread a two- or three-layer cake.

Three-Minute Sour Cream Frosting

8-ounce carton sour cream
12-ounce package cream cheese
2 cups sugar
1¼ cups water
2 egg whites
1 cup confectioners sugar
box butter cake mix for frosting

Combine sour cream with cream cheese. Boil sugar and water for 30 minutes or cook until it turns to a hard ball when dropped in water. Beat egg whites until fluffy, adding sugar solution until firm. Mix in cream cheese and sour cream mixture, and add confectioners sugar until frosting is stiff. Frosts two- to three-layer cake.

Vanilla Frosting

3 cups sugar
1¾ cups water
2 cups confectioners sugar (powdered)
2 tsp. vanilla extract
1 T. evaporated milk

In a heavy boiler, add sugar and water. Boil until syrupy, then take the assurance test: from the end of a fork, drop a small amount of syrup into ¾ cup of cold water, until it forms a round bead. Then it's ready. Remove syrup from heat. In a separate bowl, carefully beat syrup into confectioners sugar until it forms a thick frosting. Then add vanilla extract. You can add evaporated milk, if desired, to make frosting creamier or thinner. This should frost a two-layer cake.

Jelly Cake Icing

¾ cup confectioners sugar
12-ounce jar canned strawberry jelly or Mrs. Brisbon Rex's Jelly
2 single cake layers, cooled (see recipe on page 154)

In the olden days you could buy a jelly known as Rex's Jelly, which was a strawberry jelly that was good and made delicious jelly sandwiches and icing for jelly cake.

Mix confectioners sugar into jelly until all lumps disappear. Spread jelly thickly on bottom layer of cake, then place final layer on top. Ice the top layer. Do not ice sides of cake.

Mrs. Brisbon Rex's Jelly

⅓ of a 4-ounce box raspberry gelatin
¼ of a 4-ounce box strawberry gelatin
1 pound of apple jelly

Take raspberry and strawberry gelatins and stir into apple jelly. Let stand overnight. In the morning, mix well until it's smooth. Spreads two- to three-layer cakes.

Lemon Icing

1½ cups confectioners sugar
½ cup lemon juice

In a small bowl, mix and stir sugar and lemon juice with a fork until mixed well. Drip onto cool cake, and let icing stick onto cake.

Vanilla Icing

3 cups sugar
1¾ cups water
2 tsp. vanilla extract
3 egg whites, beaten until fluffy

In a heavy boiler, add sugar and water. Boil until syrupy. Then take assurance test: put a drop of syrup from the end of a fork into ¾ of a cup of cold water, until it forms a round bead. Then it's ready. Beat syrup into egg whites carefully, until fluffy and white. Then add vanilla extract.

Starr's Apple Dumpling

6 medium Delicious apples
2 pie crusts (see page 168)
2 sticks butter
2 cups sugar (plain)
2 tsp. nutmeg
½ tsp. cinnamon
1 cup brown sugar
1 cup water

Hull out the apple stems and cores, but do not cut bottom of apple away. Stuff into each apple, 1

Blackberries and dewberries grew wild along the railroad track and alongside the bushes on the sides of the road.

Berries were always known to grow in great numbers along "grudge" ditches. A late afternoon walk along the grudge ditch and railroad track was like a camp-out to all the kids, and picking berries was a joy. But, boy, do moccasins love grudge ditches! It's a wonder snakes didn't eat us alive.

Black people believed that if ever a dragonfly —or "snake doctor," as we called it—was around, a snake was nearby as well. It was said that dragonflies

tablespoon unmelted butter, 2 tablespoons plain sugar, ⅛ teaspoon nutmeg, and a sprinkle of cinnamon. Place the apples in an oblong cake pan. Add water, cover with foil, and cook for 45 minutes in the oven at 375 degrees. Remove apples and place on squares of pie crust to cover each apple over top and sides. Sprinkle brown sugar on top, place in broiling section of oven, and brown at 375 degrees. Serves 6.

Blackberry Cobbler

2 crusts (see page 159)
1½ quarts blackberries
2 tsp. vanilla
2 cups sugar
2 cups water
1½ sticks butter

In a deep boiler, place blackberries, vanilla, sugar, water, and melted butter. Simmer on stove top for 35 minutes, stirring once or twice until simmering time is complete. In a baking dish, pour one-half of the berries. Add a crust on top and brown in oven at 375 degrees. Repeat the process again, adding berries and crust, and browning again. Serve hot. Yields 8 to 10 servings.

Fresh Peach Cobbler

10 small/medium fresh peaches

3 cups water

2 cups sugar

1 stick butter or oleo

2 tsp. nutmeg or cinnamon

2 pie crusts (see page 159)

Thickening

2 T. flour

⅛ cup flour

In a deep boiler, add sliced peaches and spread sugar over top, allowing to stand for 20 to 30 minutes. Pour in water. Add butter and nutmeg. Now simmer on stove top on medium high for 60 minutes. Add one-half of thickening, or more if desired, to peaches and juice. Now add one-half of peaches to pie pan. Top with crust and brown. Add the remaining one-half of the peaches on top of browned crust. Top with final crust and brown in oven at 375 degrees.

were called "snake doctor" because snakes would eat them and be cured of whatever ailed them! As long as a snake doctor was around, you'd never find us picking dewberries. But when we didn't see snake doctors, we'd pick dewberries to our heart's (and stomach's) content.

Can't you just see us kids sticking our hands in the bushy weeds to pick dewberries, thinking we were safe because a snake doctor wasn't around? When I think about picking dewberries I am reminded of the saying "God watches over his children, and the angels of heaven protect them."

Southern Peach Cobbler

2 homemade crusts, unbaked (see page 168)
4 #303 cans peaches and juice
2 cups sugar
¾ stick butter
2 tsp. nutmeg
Thickening:
1 tsp. flour
1 T. water

In a boiler, cook peaches on top of the stove. Add sugar, butter, and nutmeg. Simmer this mixture for 60 minutes, adding the thickening at the end of the cooking period. Pour one-half of the peach mixture into a deep baking dish. Place one of the unbaked crusts on top. Brown the crust in the oven at 375 degrees. Remove from oven and add the remaining peach mixture, topping it with the second crust. Brown and serve. Yields 8 to 10 servings.

You can use the white of one egg to paint the final crust to make it crisp and crunchy. The baking dish you use for cobbler needs to be very deep. You would not use a pie pan, not even a deep-dish one. I use a granite dishpan that is about 12-inches across or a boiler. I like a round cobbler, but you could make it in a rectangular pan.

Southern Praline Pecan Pie

3 eggs
1 cup sugar
1½ cups light corn syrup
1½ tsp. vanilla
1 stick butter, melted
2 T. plain white flour
1¼ cups pecans, shelled
2 pie crusts, plain (see page 159)

Beat eggs slightly. Eggs and sugar should be creamed together until smooth. Add syrup, vanilla, and butter, mixing well. In a small dish, add flour to pecans, covering well. Pour the pecans into egg mixture. Then pour onto crust, baking for 35 to 40 minutes at 375 degrees. Serves 6 to 7 persons.

Lemon Ice Box Pie

4 eggs, separated, yolks and whites
1 6-ounce can sweetened condensed milk
juice of 4 lemons
7-ounce box of vanilla wafers

Place egg yolks in bowl and beat slightly, adding condensed milk until mixed well. Pour in lemon juice slowly, alternating with condensed milk, stirring constantly until the mixture is thick enough to stand. Take three-fourths box of vanilla wafers and roll into crumbs for bottom of pie. Line edge of pie plate with vanilla wafers, pour in the lemon juice and condensed milk filling, and top with meringue (See meringue recipe on page 167.) Yields 6 slices.

Mama's Double Apple Pie

6 large Delicious apples, peeled
4 cups water
¾ stick butter
1½ tsp. cinnamon
2⅓ cups sugar
1 tsp. nutmeg
Thickening:
2 T. plain white flour
1 cup water
2 layers of crust (see page 168)

Wash, peel, and cut apples into slices or wedges. Place in a boiler, adding water, butter, cinnamon, sugar and nutmeg. Simmer on the stove top for 60 minutes. Add flour thickening, and allow to simmer for 15 additional minutes. Pour one-half of mixture into pie pan. Cover with crust and brown at 375 degrees. Pour final one-half of mixture onto crust and top with second crust, browning at 375 degrees. Cool and serve with vanilla ice cream to make Apple Pie a la Mode if desired. Serves 6 to 7.

Meringue

  3 egg whites
  ¼ cup sugar

Place egg whites in bowl and beat at high speed until they begin to turn fluffy. Alternate sugar while beating until stiff.

Tips on perfect meringues

Never let any yolk get into the whites. It will cause the egg whites to fall. Do not put too much sugar in meringue or it will be watery or lose stiffness. Do not leave in oven over 1 to 2 minutes. Sugar browns fast.

Pie Crust

2 cups plain white flour, sifted
1 cup vegetable shortening
¼ cup water
dash of salt

Pour flour into bowl, adding shortening and water, with a dash of salt. Stir with fork until shortening, salt, and water are mixed in with flour. Do not add any more flour than needed to form dough. Too much flour will make crust tough. Roll out to sizes that will fit two 9-inch pie plates. Crinkle edges, pour in filling and bake at 375 degrees for the amount of time it takes to cook the filling.

Garden Fresh
Upper Ground Potatoes
(also known as Jerusalem artichokes)

2 9-inch pie crusts (see above)
4 medium upper ground potatoes
2½ quarts water
2 cups sugar
2 T. nutmeg or cinnamon, as preferred

3 eggs
2 T. baking powder
½ cup evaporated milk

In a large boiler, boil "potatoes" for 60 minutes or until tender. Drain. In a bowl, mash until all lumps are gone. Add nutmeg, eggs, milk and baking powder. Stir well until all ingredients are thoroughly mixed. Now add sugar, stirring into potatoes carefully. Pour onto pie crust. You should have enough mixture to fill two pie crusts. Bake in oven for 60 minutes at 350 degrees. Serves 6 to 7 persons.

There are many delicious ways to cook the upper ground potatoes. They are also good boiled, with just a little salt and pepper and butter.

Sweet Potato Pie

5 medium sweet potatoes
3 to 4 quarts water
1¼ sticks butter, melted
1½ cups sugar
2½ tsp. nutmeg
2 tsp. vanilla
3 eggs
1½ T. baking powder
⅓ cups evaporated milk

My great-grandfather, David Fleming, had two "sweet potato pumps," one for the family to use for daily cooking, and the other for him to store his seed potatoes. He would save the very best potatoes (everybody loved the big red Puerto Rico yams) and put them in a special "pump." They would pile the potatoes up in a pyramid and cover them over, first with dirt and hay, and then with croker or gunny sacks (burlap) so the air and cold could not get in. Then they would put up poles around the pump, and place tin across the top to keep out the rain. Nobody was allowed to go in this pump, so the potatoes would be just right for planting in the spring.

Wash and peel sweet potatoes. Place in deep boiler, covering with water. Simmer for 60 minutes until ready for mashing. Cream potatoes, removing all lumps. Add butter, sugar, nutmeg, vanilla, and eggs, mixing well. Add baking powder to milk, and stir into potatoes. Pour ingredients into pie shells and bake at 350 degrees for 50 minutes or until firm. Cool and serve. Yields 12 to 14 slices.

Layered Sweet Potato Pie

homemade crust (see page 168)
5 cups water
6 medium sweet potatoes
2¾ cups sugar
2 tsp. vanilla
2½ tsp. nutmeg
1 stick pure butter

Wash and slice sweet potatoes. Place in water, adding sugar, vanilla, nutmeg, and butter. Simmer until slightly candied. Place half of potatoes in pie pan, topping with a crust, and brown at 375 degrees. Then add another layer of potatoes and crust. Brown. Yields 12 servings. Takes about 45 to 55 minutes to brown.

Sweet Potatoes and Marshmallow Bake

5 medium sweet potatoes
1 stick butter
2½ tsp. nutmeg
2 tsp. vanilla
1 cup raisins
1½ cups sugar
3 eggs
⅛ cup evaporated milk
1½ T. baking powder
3 cups marshmallows
3 quarts water

Peel and slice sweet potatoes. Place in a boiler with water, simmering until tender for 1½ hours. Strain potatoes, place in bowl, adding butter, and mash until all lumps are removed and potatoes are smooth. Add nutmeg, vanilla, raisins, sugar, eggs, evaporated milk, and baking powder. Stir all ingredients into potatoes carefully. Place in bread pan, cooking with marshmallows on top for 1 hour at medium heat. Serves 10 to 12.

Sweet potatoes were one of the widely grown sweets among southerners and many uses were found for them. We always considered sweet potatoes a dessert.

Sometimes the fields would produce so many potatoes my grandmama had to cook potatoes all kinds of different ways. She had all the children grating potatoes.

Sweet Potato Pone

5 sweet potatoes, peeled and grated
1½ cups sugar
2 tsp. baking powder
3 eggs
1 stick butter
3 tsp. vanilla
nutmeg, if desired

Wash and grate sweet potatoes, adding sugar, baking powder, eggs, butter, vanilla, and nutmeg. Place in baking pan. Bake for 1½ hours at 375 degrees. Cool and serve. Serves 6 to 7 persons.

Candied Yams (Sweet Potatoes)

6 medium sweet potatoes
2 quarts water
2 tsp. nutmeg
2¾ cups sugar
1½ sticks butter

Wash and slice sweet potatoes oblong. Place in pan with water, sprinkling nutmeg and sugar on top. Cut up butter evenly on top and simmer for 1½ hours until tender. Serves 8 to 10.

Starr's Banger

¼ cup rum
1 cup orange juice
1 tsp. vanilla flavor extract
½ tsp. sugar
crushed ice
2 cherries with stems

Place in pitcher, rum, orange juice, vanilla, and sugar. Mix well. Serve in tall glasses with crushed ice, and top with a cherry. Serves drinks for 2.

Orange and Pineapple Sherbert Punch

1 16-ounce can pineapple juice
½ gallon ginger ale
1 box gelatin
½ gallon pineapple sherbert
½ gallon orange sherbert

Combine pineapple juice, ginger ale, and gelatin, mixing well. Add both sherberts to drink mixture and serve. Yields 20 to 25 6-ounce glasses of punch.

This is a dessert for gatherings, summer picnics, weddings, anything festive. Watermelons are at their best in the summertime when they are not expensive. You can omit any of the fruits you desire, and use more of others.

Watermelon Basket

1 large watermelon, 15 to 16 pounds
  (cube part of watermelon)
2 sliced oranges, trimmed for decor
2 cups canteloupe, cubed
2 cups honeydew melon, cubed
1 cup grapes
½ cup cherries
2 cups strawberries
½ cup sweet apple chunks
1 cup orange slices, peeled
2 T. Fruit Fresh (preservative of color)
1 cup confectioners sugar

With a wedge-cutting knife, split the watermelon, cutting it in the shape of a basket with a handle. Leave two inches of watermelon in the hollows of the watermelon basket. Decorate the watermelon by cutting crinkles around the edge and sides. Place cubed canteloupes, watermelon, honeydew melon, grapes, cherries, strawberries, oranges, apples, fruit preservative, and sugar into basket. Decorate with orange slices for wagon wheel appearance. Chill and serve. Serves 20 persons.

Ambrosia

8 oranges sliced (skin removed)
1 jar cherries, drained
1 can coconut, moist
¾ cup sugar
1½ cups pineapple
2 cups skinless grapes (canned)

In bowl, add oranges, juices, cherries, coconut, sugar, pineapple, and grapes. Mix well, chill in refrigerator, and serve. Yields 8 to 10 4-ounce bowls.

Egg Nog

4 egg yolks
1 cup sugar
1 pint cream
2 tsp. nutmeg
1 tsp. vanilla
1½ cups bourbon or brandy
½ cup sweet milk

In a bowl, beat egg yolks, and cream in sugar. Beat cream until fluffy. Add to egg mixture, and stir in nutmeg, vanilla, liquor of choice, and milk. Chill and serve. Yields 6 to 8 glasses.

Kathy's Favorite Everyday Dinners

First Week

Monday
Fried Chicken
Rice/Gravy
Green Peas
Dinner Rolls
Iced Tea

Tuesday
Fried Porkchops
Creamed Potatoes/Gravy
Mustard Greens
Corn Bread

Wednesday
Sirloin Steak
Rice/Gravy
Green Beans Sauté
Corn Bread

Thursday
Spaghetti with Meat Sauce
Green Tossed Salad
Dinner Rolls

Friday
Fried Catfish
Potato Salad
Corn Bread

Saturday
Grilled Steak
Baked Potato/Sour Cream
and Butter
Green Salad
Dinner Rolls

Sunday
Baked Duck
Dressing with Giblet Gravy
Potato Salad
Green Peas
Cranberry Sauce
Dinner Rolls

Desserts
Lemon Glazed Cake
Sweet Potato Pie

Beverage
Iced Tea

176

Second Week

Monday
Vegetable Soup/Stew Meat
Corn Bread

Tuesday
Baked Chuck Roast
Creamed Potato/Gravy
Butter Beans
Corn Bread

Wednesday
Baked Chicken
Rice/Gravy
Collard Greens/Hock Bones
Corn Bread

Thursday
Liver/Onion Gravy
Creamed Potatoes
Black-Eyed Peas
Corn Bread

Friday
Chicken and Dumplings
Green Salad
Rolls

Saturday
Chitterlings
Potato Salad
Corn Bread
Hot Sauce/Ketchup

Sunday
Baked Ham
Candied Sweet Potatoes
Potato Salad
Dinner Rolls
Green Beans with Potatoes

Dessert
Lemon Meringue Pie

Beverage
Iced Tea

Kathy's Party Specials

Dinner Party

Red Beans/Rice
Orange Glazed Duck
Duck Dressing
Potato Salad
Cranberries (whole)
Fried Catfish
Chitterlings
Corn Bread
Rolls

Hot Tamales
Cheese/Ham Tray
Tuna Fish Salad

Watermelon Basket
Sweet Potato Pie
Caramel Cake

Beer
Wine
Tea
Soda

Heavenly Seafood Bash

Maine Lobster, Broiled over
Rice Hills

Seafood Gumbo with Rice
Fried Catfish and Potato Salad
Southern Red Beans and Rice

Shrimp Etouffée
Fried Oysters
Broiled Crab Legs
Shrimp Cocktail

Corn Bread
Party-Style Crackers

Kathy's Home Remedies

During my childhood, many remedies were used for various illnesses, some of which were logical and others that seemed obnoxious. Whether they made sense or not, for one reason or the other they seemed to work.

General Healing

Blacks believed that fresh greens from the garden were a healing food.

Measles, Other Childhood Illnesses

During the days of outbreaks of childhood illnesses like measles, shuck teas were made for bringing out the measles and therefore curing the ailment. 3 to 5 corn shucks, 2 tsp. sugar, 1 pint of water and a pinch of mint leaf, if desired, for palatability.

In a boiler add shucks, sugar, and water, boiling for 1 hour or until the water turns to a tea colored brown. Add a mint leaf, if desired, for a smoother taste.

Chest and Head Colds

Tallow was used for colds, just like Vick's Salve was used to cure chest and head colds. Here is how to make tallow. You will need these things.:

　　an old tin can
　　2 cups old discarded grease
　　Plastic covering

In a can, place all grease and cover, allowing to sit out for 2 to 3 weeks, or until grease has tallowed.

Malaria

During the summer season, outbreaks of malaria would occur. The old remedy used was quinine tablets and tea.

Mumps

Sardines were always a regular for the mumps. You would take the oil of the sardines and rub from neck up to the chin and ears, then tie the jaws up with a white rag. Black families believed the rag kept the mumps from going down on boys and relieved the pressure on the gland area. The sardines would be eaten after rubbing with the oil.

High Blood Pressure

Vinegar and garlic were used for high blood pressure. Blacks believed that they could eat salt and pork as desired, and drink a solution of vinegar with garlic after eating, and it would keep the blood pressure down.

Preventing Lockjaw

If a child stepped on an nail, you would take a piece of fat meat and tie a rag around the area. The fat meat would draw out the poison and keep the child from developing lockjaw.

Coughing

Honey, lemon, and a whiskey tonic would stop coughs.

Cleaning Teeth

When I was a child, people believed in cleaning teeth with a sassafras twig, salt, or baking soda and water instead of with the fancy toothpaste one couldn't afford.

Sore Throat and Thrush

When a child got sore throat or thrush, the older folks believed that rinsing the throat with one's own urine healed the sore throat or thrush.

Mouthwash

The mouthwash blacks would use was an old mouth freshener, called Sen-Sen. It looked like small black, flat pellets and had minty root-beer type taste that would flow throughout the mouth. The smell was soothing.

Sores

Soot and cobwebs were used to put on sores. They were packed down with tallow, and in two or three days, the sore was well.

Index

J

Jellies:
  Mrs. Brisbon Rex's jelly, 160
  plum, 129–130
Jelly cake icing, 159–60
Jerusalem artichoke pie, 168–69

K

Kidney beans, 96–97

L

Layered sweet potato pie, 170
Lemon broiled fish, 73
Lemon ice box pie, 165–66
Lemon icing, 160
Lemon rind pound cake, 155–56
Lemon whiskey sauce, 153
Lima beans, Mama's, 97
Lobster, stuffed, 76
Lye hominy, 107

M

Macaroni and cheese, 86
Macaroni salad, 122–23
Mama's double apple pie, 166–67
Mama's lima beans, 97
Meatloaf, 27
Menus, 4, 54, 92, 139, 176–78
Meringue, 167
Mixed squirrel sausage, 48–49

Miz Augustine's oven-baked chicken, 61–62
Miz Bob's buffalo fish, 70
Miz Laura's yeast rolls, 145–46
Mrs. Brisbon Rex's jelly, 160
Mrs. Hunter's Southern tea cakes, 149
Mustard and turnip greens, mixed, 104–5

N

Neckbone and macaroni stew, 37
Nutty cream cheese frosting, 157–58

O

Okra:
  boiled, 108
  Southern fried, 108
Old fashioned egg custard, 149–50
Omelet, ham and egg, 83
Orange and pineapple sherbet punch, 173
Orange glazed duck, 66–67
Oysters:
  Delta-fried, 77
  oyster loaf, 77–78
Oven-baked barbecued chicken, 57–58
Oven-baked coon with yams, 43
Oven-baked deer ham, 46
Oven-baked pork and beans, 98

P

Peach brandy, 132–33
Peach cobbler, 163—164
Peach preserves, 131